It Happens As We Speak

a feminist poetics

The power of art to create connections denied by the intellect working alone, to transform the unnameable into something palpable, sensuous, visible, audible, to take our unexpressed thoughts and desires and fling them with clarity and coherence on the wall, a screen, a sheet of paper, or against the long silence of history—this power has been instinctively recognized by women as a key to our deepest political problem: our deprivation of the power to name. In beginning to create art which claims this right, we begin to create a politics which is a critique of all existing culture, and all existing politics.
ADRIENNE RICH

Pat Falk

Plain View Press
P. O. 42255
Austin, TX 78704

plainviewpress.net
sbright1@austin.rr.com
512-441-2452
512-440-7139 (fax)

It Happens As We Speak

a feminist poetics

Copyright Pat Falk, 2006. All rights reserved.
ISBN: 978-1-891386-55-8
Library of Congress Number: 2006904031

Cover art Miriam Schapiro, *Anonymous No More?* 1996, acrylic, paper collage, 21 x 29 3/8" (text: Adrienne Rich)

Back cover photo of Pat Falk by Karen-Kluges Stolberg.

Contents

Acknowledgments	7
Prologue	9
According to this Necessity	15
A Spy in the House of Ed	21
The Death of a Beautiful Woman	29
The Madwoman in the Attic	39
The Day the Music Died	47
Today Life Opened Inside Me	53
A Life I Didn't Choose	59
In a Time of Violence	69
Remembering Jane	77
The Gilded Cage	83
The Flow of Knowledge	91
Inside, Looking	99
Notes	105
About the Author	115

Acknowledgements

Several people have read and responded to this manuscript at different stages; my thanks go to Michael Anzalone, Carol Farber, Beth Fein, Oriole Farb-Feshbach, Annie Finch, Niamh Fitzgerald, Barbara Hofman, Gary Ivan, Hedda Marcus, Mary Miceli, Patricia Monaghan, Alicia Ostriker, Molly Peacock and Pramila Venkateswaren. Jean Henning of the Nassau County Museum of Art, and Beth Levinthal and Jerene Weitman of the Heckscher Museum of Art, provided valuable research and other assistance. Special thanks to Pratt Institute of Art, for providing support through their graduate internship program and particularly to Marilyn Lyons, Associate Professor and Internship Coordinator, and to Karen Kluges-Stolberg, Graduate Intern, Communication Design, for her intelligence, skill, and patient assistance. My deep appreciation to Susan Bright for her interest and commitment. Finally, my love to Karen Anna, Tammy Brady, Beth Fein, Sidney Feshbach, Adrienne Rich, and Gloria Wygand—their support has made all the difference.

For permission to reprint previously published text, either in part or in full, I'd like to thank Trio Press, Halifax, Canada, for "I Had to Leave a Little Girl," originally published in *Like a Second Mother: Nannies and Housekeepers in the Lives of Wealthy Children*, 1999; Midmarch Arts Press, New York, for permission to reprint my review (1994) of Jane Cooper's *Scaffolding*; the Sophia Center, Huntington, N.Y. for "A Conversation with Eavan Boland"; Canio's Editions for "Abortion," from *In the Shape of a Woman* (1995). Passages of poetry by Eavan Boland reprinted by permission of Eavan Boland; Passages of Jane Cooper's poetry from *The Flashboat: Poems Collected and Reclaimed* by Jane Cooper. Copyright (c) 2000 by Jane Cooper. Used by permission of W.W. Norton & Company, Inc. "Cancion," by Denise Levertov, from *The Freeing of the Dust*, copyright (c) 1975 by Denise Levertov. Reprinted by permission of New Directions Publishing Corp.; "Song for Ishtar" by Denise Levertov, from *Poems 1960-1967*, copyright (c) 1966 by Denise Levertov. Reprinted by permission of New Directions Publishing Corp.; "Growth of a Poet" by Denise Levertov from *Poems 1972-1982*, copyright (c) 1975 by Denise Levertov reprinted by permission of New Directions Publishing Corp. Passages of Sylvia Plath's poetry from "Three Women: A Poem for Three Voices" from *Winter Trees* Copyright (c) 1968 by Ted Hughes and lines from "The Hanging Man" from *Ariel* Copyright (c) 1965 by Ted Hughes. Reprinted by permission of HarperCollins Publishers; passages of Anne Sexton's poetry from *The Complete Poems by Anne Sexton*. Copyright (c) 1981 by Linda G. Sexton reprinted by permission of Houghton Mifflin Company. All rights reserved. While every effort has been made to trace and obtain permission from copyright holders, we would be pleased to hear from any not here acknowledged.

Prologue

City College, New York, 1974

Adrienne Rich offers me a piece of chocolate from the Hershey bar she has just unwrapped. We are in the faculty lounge of the English Department. I called her a few weeks ago at her home, introduced myself, and asked if I could borrow her copy of *A Change of World*; it's out of print and I need to read it before I start writing my honor's thesis on her poetry. She was very kind, agreeing to lend me the book, suggesting that we meet in her office the next day. Since then I've been auditing her course, "Images of Women in the Poetry of Men," talking with her frequently.

"Thank you," I say, slipping the thin square of chocolate on to my tongue. We walk out of the lounge and down the hall.

"You know," I continue, "I have come to consider you my literary mother."

"I felt that way about Simone de Beauvoir," Adrienne responds.

"That means I'm part of a feminist literary tradition..!"

"I suppose you can say that."

Lindenhurst, March 2, 1997

I'm on sabbatical.

The word *sabbatical* is related to *sabbath*: rest, reflection, meditation. Like keeping the sabbath day, like lighting a candle. I must take time from work, note change with ritual, let go.

An old dream: I'm on the shore, holding on to the rope of a boat which is being thrust and bumped against the bulkhead, then pulled out toward the sea on huge cresting waves. The thick rope cuts into my palms.

I am bleeding and can't hold on any longer.

And if I let go? Maybe the boat will sail off to some great adventure; maybe it will be smashed. But my power is not nearly as great as some other force—wind, tide, current—a magnificent beast that presides on earth.

I let go of the boat and it's thrown on to the waves. I'm alone, standing on expansive, shifting sand.

Another image: I am the boat. I let the winds and tide take me out.

Writing requires a leap of faith: in myself, language, art, music, in the daily rhythms and currents of life. This is labor, different than work. In the morning, when my mind is most clear and focused, I leisurely putter, clean up the house, move from book to desk to a poem to a page of this manuscript; walk my dog, have breakfast; drive to the beach.

Where sea meets land is the place of change: solid becomes soft, soft becomes liquid; liquid, firm; shape, form, solid, stone. Boats are stones, winged with sails.

I am reflecting on ideas, images and processes that I have valued, perhaps clung to, for much of my life; reflecting on change; and changing. I am trying to locate who I am as a woman and a writer in the world. It will happen as I speak.

April 14, 1997

I visited the Nassau County Museum of Art, saw the exhibit *The Feminine Image*. On the way out, I purchased the catalogue, in order to return to the paintings, photographs and sculpture, and to read the essays. Donald Kuspit, in the introduction to the catalogue, notes that "the irony of many woman-made works is that they reject man's double vision of her...but without the expected result of independent identity...standing on her own, without the support of man's desire for her—woman seems peculiarly limited and bereft, and more isolated than independent."

Bereft? No, sad. On the shore, working, digging my feet into the sand, walking inland, turning around, re-rooting, gazing out to sea—of course I want to be desired; I need the kind of intimacy, companionship and support that enable all of us to flourish.

Must I reject the male perception of me? Connect artistically, sexually, only with women? I do know that I need to support and be supported by other women, other artists of integrity and passion.

I must also live a consciously political life among people who see beyond a binary vision of any human being. While remaining open to multiple perspectives, I must negate when necessary, affirm when possible, but always challenge.

I must turn inward, so deeply that I forget myself.

I must take action. With others.

I am changing the pronoun in the title of this manuscript from *I* to *We*. *It Happens As We Speak: Notes Toward a Feminization of Form*.

How much, as a child, I wanted to challenge authority. I couldn't wait to grow up, determined to write a book that would expose what was going on in my family. Later I wanted to challenge my professors, especially those who forbade the use of the word "feminist" in my academic essays, or those who insisted I write in disembodied, inhuman prose. But speaking up to—or against—our parents, teachers, lovers, government—needs to be balanced by close examination of ourselves, individually and collectively.

Because I find myself part of the traditions and institutions I am challenging, it becomes more vital than ever to look at myself, my own patterns and postures; to take responsibility for my creativity; change what I can.

Lindenhurst, April 18, 1997

The roots of my isolation go far back: to growing up in a family from which I needed to estrange myself; to a tendency to forge masks, create walls; to the child who used language to conceal and reveal. To the young girl who couldn't understand why she was chronically ill with a disease that would years later be diagnosed as autoimmune disorder; to that lost young girl who, through a bizarre complex of associations, imagined herself to be a young college student who died and was dismembered in the hands of her doctor after a botched abortion.

To the young schoolgirl who never lived up to what she was told was her "academic potential"; who was never popular like the girls with long straight blond hair, the thin ones, the pretty ones. To the young woman who acted dumb and cute in the company of men in order to appear feminine.

To the young woman in college, in graduate school, who became an "honor student," it seemed, out of pretense, faking enthusiasm and intelligence in order to get an A—while writing poetry "on her own." To the woman who in marriage gave up her name and spirit, seeking various sources of comfort to heal the continuing rupturing wounds.

≈

There is also the woman who has spent the last decade creating a safe, stable environment for herself and her daughter, finding that a rented house, overlooking a river that goes out to sea, could hold her, nurture her, protect her, inspire her. The woman-poet who has twice been given the gift of sabbatical to reflect, write, publish; who is learning about friendship, healing.

♒

No, the artist need not be isolated from the world. That's an old destructive myth. But there are periods of isolation, inevitable loneliness and loss. There is also a need to re-perceive, re-make, re-define myself, my poetics; and then there is the coming out, the saying of the truth that is the only path toward integrity, dignity, and community.

This has happened in women's writing. As we continue to explore, challenge, open, speak—images of isolation change. We have become engaged in a process, individually and collectively, changing perceptions of ourselves *within and apart from* the community of men.

I began my own search for an authentic voice intuitively as a child; more consciously in the mid-seventies while an undergraduate studying literature at The City College of New York, focusing on the theme of "the problem of the artist." I asked Adrienne Rich, then a visiting professor, if being a woman-poet was a central concern for her at that time.

Yes.

We walked together across campus the day after Anne Sexton killed herself, talking on the way to the lecture hall where Adrienne would address the college community, where she would speak about our responsibilities as women and as poets.

"What are you planning to do after you graduate?" she asked, turning around to face me before we entered the building.

"Continue in grad school, I guess."

"The institution will fuck you up."

Is this what it means to be part of a feminist literary tradition? Why did Adrienne say that to me? Will the institution make me crazy? Pregnant? Fucked up?

Later, in graduate school, I approached a professor regarding my plans for a Ph. D. dissertation. When I said that I wanted to write on feminist poetics, I was forbidden to use the word *feminist*.

So I developed a strategy of circumvention and re-invention, re-casting the term, "feminist poetics" into the process, *the feminization of form*. I came up with a definition: *the movement from internalization, assimilation and mimesis of a patriarchal creative process to an organic rooting in authentic female sensibility and its formalization in language.*

Good. I had a starting point. I wasn't sure what I meant by a "patriarchal" (male?) "creative process," but I sensed that it had something to do with polarity, binary thinking, hierarchy, institutionalized logic. It often embodied misogynist attitudes and assumptions about women and women's creativity. I knew that I had to speak about the repression of wisdom—*Sophia*—of nature, instinct, multiplicity, matter: not necessarily essential female qualities, but as entities historically associated with female qualities, thus devalued, often destroyed.

To be clear: polarity and misogyny are not synonymous, yet they seem to negatively support and intensify each other, perpetuating dangerous assumptions regarding gender and the creative process, contributing to the split sensibility and pain I have seen in my literary mothers and in myself. One of the most dangerous splits: the male principle as active agent, spirit, thought; the female principle as passive matter; the formative process resulting from the synthesis of these two polarities. Yin/Yang, Anima/Animus, Structure/Form. To feminize form, we have had to transform that sensibility, that split.

∽∽

Adrienne Rich asks in "Notes Toward a Politics of Location,"

> Is there a connection between this state of mind—the cold war mentality, the attribution of all our problems to an external enemy—and a form of feminism so focused on male evil and female victimization that it, too, allows for no differences among women, men, places, times, cultures, conditions, classes, movements? Living in the climate of an enormous either/or, we absorb some of it unless we actively take heed.

Multiplicity, inclusiveness, and what has sometimes been referred to as "women's ways of knowing" are often invoked as Post Modern antidotes to an either/or perception. A kind of Keatsian *negative capability*: to be in "uncertainties, mysteries, doubts, without any irritable reaching after fact and reason."

But how then to focus? How to stay grounded with so much sensory input? Where, indeed, to locate a center? Without a familiar dualistic pattern of polarities and the dialectical process they engender, how can we create paradigms that embody female form?

The process, *the feminization of form*, must be tracked not only through a direct observance of specific traditional poetic forms, such as the sonnet or ode; or the formal arrangement of words, lines, stanzas; but also through what Annie Finch refers to as "experimental" and "imported" forms that enable us to embody organic female energy and rhythms. This becomes a "new kind of formal poetics...radical formalism, tribal or root postmodernism."

Most fully—and what I examine in this poetics—we need to explore the peripheral stage of creation where process and substance merge, where the verb *to form* becomes the noun, *form*.

Amityville, September 16, 2003

Of all places! A yard sale! I found a book by Jane Mills, *Womanwords: A Dictionary of Words About Women*, published in 1989. I'm drawn to her discussion of the history of the word, *focus*. In Latin, the word means "hearth, fireplace, pyre, altar or, used figuratively, a home." Mills connects the meaning of the word to the Roman goddess of the hearth, Vesta, adopted from the Greek *Hestia*. She quotes from Patricia Monaghan's *Women in Myth and Legend*:

> "Living at the centre of every home [Hestia]...symbolized family unity and, by extension, as goddess of the public hearth, she embodied the social contract. In the beginning of her worship, matrilineal succession seems to have been the rule, and traces of it survived in the custom of classical Greece whereby a new home was not considered established until a woman brought fire from her mother's hearth to light her own. In the same way, Greek colonists brought fire from the mother city's public hearth to assure the cohesion of their new communities."

A woman's center—organic, rhythmic, cohesive. An individual journey within the journey of many.

It is how this poetics has taken shape.

According to this Necessity

> *Nobody can counsel and help you, nobody. There is
> only one single way. Go into yourself. Search for
> the reason that bids you write...ask yourself in the
> stillest hour of your night: must I write...
> then build your life according to this necessity...*
>   Rilke, Letters to a Young Poet

Jamaica Estates, 1954

I am living in a house on the service road of Grand Central Parkway near 188th Street, in Jamaica Estates. It is two blocks from the grammar school I'll be starting next year—P.S. 178. In a few months, we'll move around the corner to a bigger house on Avon Road, where I'll have my own room. In the room I share now with my little sister Denise, is our own television. I love *The Sandy Becker Show*, especially the parts where children at home are magically transported into the television studio. I hope that when the time comes for us to get sucked into the television to be on the show, we will be wearing nice pajamas. On nasty days we play in the basement, that's where I have my birthday parties. On good days we dig in the back yard to get to China, or look for gold stones in the driveway.

My father is a lawyer, and he goes to court a lot. My mother is a sometimes swirling haze of crinkly, satiny material and sweet smelling perfume. At other times she is ugly: crashing on dexedrine, groggy from seconals, recovering from one of several shock treatments or attempted suicides. I need to be careful not to do something bad or say something wrong, or to laugh out loud, which disturbs my mother. Then I will get a beating.

I don't know much about courage, or my place in this house, and I don't understand the sense of quiet terror and control that permeates the air.

One afternoon I startle myself, and speak out in a voice that is foreign to me, a voice that is clear, direct, sure. My older sister Adrienne, who is six, is sitting at the piano, reciting for the piano teacher, Mr. Breed. When the lesson is over, and my mother enters the room, I make my presence known. I have been sitting on the steps that descend into the front foyer, a few feet from the living room where the lessons are given.

"I want piano lessons."

Suddenly I sense space—and a window, through which six eyes are looking in: my mother's, Mr. Breed's, and my sister's.

"You've been listening all this time?" Mr. Breed asks.
"Yes, every week."
"Have you learned anything?"
"A quart of milk gets one beat."

I will later learn the correct words, *a quarter note* gets one beat. My attention is focused on the word, *beat,* however; and a quarter note and a quart of milk are one and the same in my language center. Notes are milk, creamy and sweet. Beat means rhythm, not pain. Or maybe all the beats are tied up together. But there is one beat that I like, that feels good. It is the beat of music.

〰〰

It became a family joke, my linguistic mix-up, but the joke never cut into the respect I gained from my mother and piano teacher that one afternoon. It was, for me, the first time I verbalized desire so directly and with such clarity and authority. It was also the first time I recall using language poetically: a semantic overlap, a synapse, became a way to transform pain. From then on, poetry served as a vehicle through which my perceptions and spirit moved; the rest of me acting out a myriad of roles determined and constructed by circumstance.

〰〰

Jamaica Estates, 1955

I like this new house. It is made of brick and stone, one of hundreds of Tudors spread throughout the neighborhood. It is nestled high up on a hill, surrounded by a rolling green lawn and gardens in the spring. Lilacs and roses and forsythia. Sprouts of Honeysuckle that really taste good.

My father says that the hills were formed by glaciers. The hill that goes from Avon Road down to Kent is great for roller skating, and the hill that goes from Avon to Chevy Chase is great for sledding in the winter. I have a Flexible Flier. The best ride begins on the top of the sloping lawn, packed with snow. When I land on the street, I turn left down Avon, then left again on to Chevy Chase, down two blocks past Radnor to Midland Parkway. Then I have to stop, pull back the front hand brakes (with frozen fists) because there are always lots of cars on Midland Parkway.

Another thing I love to do: chop rocks. Along the walkway on the side of the house are Azalea bushes. I crawl under and pull out all different shapes and sizes of stones, usually grey or dirty brown. Then I find a huge rock and pound the littler ones until they crack open into jagged pieces. I am amazed, thrilled at the beauty inside: silver mica, white mountainous ridges, glittering gold in the sunlight. I always put the brilliant pieces back under the bushes for safe keeping.

〰

There's a cat that comes around here all the time. My mother won't let me bring her inside, so I put milk and tuna fish out for her. I named her Tammy, from the song. Something about cotton fields, whispering, love. *Taaaaaaa-mee's in love.* There's a place in my mind where words and sounds just swim around and I hear them even when everything is quiet. Maybe it's the place where everything that's invisible lives. I wish I could live there. I wish I could keep this cat, I'm really worried what will happen to her in the winter. Maybe her family hits her. Maybe she is running away.

〰

Sometimes my father takes me into his law office in Manhattan, an hour's drive in his Cadillac from Queens. At 225 Broadway, on the 31st floor overlooking the Hudson River, I am allowed to sit at the secretary's desk and play with the electric typewriter. The keyboard is complicated: the letter *w* takes up five spaces, the letter *l*, two, so I have to learn how many spaces each letter occupies when back-spacing to erase with correct-type. I am becoming confident mastering the numerical system of this machine, while comforted and excited by the rhythm of the keys striking the page, just as my fingers strike the keys and make music on the piano. But now, instead of music, out come words, words in a rhythm, words sounding like they come from a song. Words and letters that take up space, make arrangements on a white page.

Hear the ringing of the bells, of the bells bells bells bells bells bells bells, the ringing and the singing of the bells! So this is the secret behind Poe's poem, the poem that I read out loud over and over again, sitting on my bed in my room. Sometimes I gaze through the window overlooking the back yard, staring at the night sky, imagining the universe, pondering the impossibility of its limits. There is a deep mystery, something that needs to be answered: the universe has to end somewhere, but it doesn't.

There is another mystery, something else that needs to be answered, about my family. The chaos. The pain. The violence.

Somehow it all seems connected with something I saw in my father's office. I wandered into the library, taking down huge leather volumes of books, all on boring legal issues, many dealing with car accidents and negligence. A series of photographs in one of them grips my imagination: in a chapter titled "Trauma" are three photographs of one woman in different poses. In all three she is naked, covered with several wounds, scars, and bruises. And she is awfully fat, so fat that her breasts hang down over the overlapping layers of her belly, on to her wide-spread thighs, covering what I know must be her vagina. I am fascinated, disgusted, fascinated. What, I wonder, does this poor miserable woman stuck in a book have to do with beautiful letters and words arranged in space on white paper, with the rhythm of the white and black keys of a piano; the rhythm of my fingers typing, striking, flying across the keys of a typewriter, the rhythm of the bells bells bells bells bells bells bells, of the ringing and the singing of the bells?

≈

I believed that school would give me answers. My earliest exposure to textbooks taught me that Jane wore a red coat. School also taught me to crouch under my desk during an air raid drill. School taught me that there was a thing called government, that there was such a thing as poetry that existed outside my bedroom, but that it was different from a composition. In fifth grade, we had a monthly assignment to write either a poem or a composition about the month—I always wrote a poem—and at the end of the school year, we gathered them into a folder for viewing by our parents, who were to come to open school night.

I was surprised that my mother came. She said she liked the poems, but why didn't I write anything else? I don't recall my mother ever coming to school after that. She was busy. Or sick. Or in the mental institution. I don't remember my father ever coming to school. He was busy with his law practice, he was running for congress, he wanted to be a judge. He belonged to several organizations, including The Boy Scouts of America, The Sea Scouts, The Family Service League, the democratic party. I was later to work for him, doing secretarial duties, campaigning for candidates I knew nothing about.

My father also belonged to the Jewish War Veterans. He had been a Commander in the Navy during World War II, leading a fleet of ships during the Invasion of Normandy, receiving the purple heart for one of his wounds. Once I found in his den a *Time-Life* book, large and flat, of images from the war, including photographs of the concentration camps. In black and white bodies were piled one on top of another, naked, and I spent hours trying to untangle an arm, a leg, a head, genitals. These images, and those of the fat woman in the Trauma book, were the first I saw of the exposed human body, besides my own.

〜

By junior high I was writing more prose than poetry: book reports and research papers; the poetry I kept to myself. Once, though, after reading Coleridge's "The Rime of the Ancient Mariner," we were assigned to write a poem dealing with the five senses. When I mentioned this to my mother, she said she wanted to write it and have me give it to my teacher, pretending it was mine, just to see what the teacher would say. I did as she asked. The teacher loved the poem and put it up on the bulletin board. I recall the repeated refrain, *how blind are they that cannot see*. Why don't you own up to your own stuff, I wanted to ask my mother. Why did you stop writing? You used to write poetry. You started a novel once, remember, those months you spent in Payne Whitney? I found the manuscript in the dining room, was impressed how vividly you described the scene playing badminton on the hospital grounds. You used a different name than your own—*Lillian* became *Lenora*—but you kept the first letter.

I knew it was you.

A Spy in the House of Ed

> *I begin thinking about political theory by thinking about the way we think. I speculate about ideology. About form...the forms of hierarchies, of institutions, of habits, the way things are done; the forms of language, gesture, art, of thought, and equally, of emotion...*
> Susan Griffin, "The Way of All Ideology"

*The Graduate School and University Center,
City University of New York, September, 1977*

I must come up with a dissertation topic, and am pulled in two directions. First, because I see myself as a novice feminist critic in the midst of a conservative, traditional university, I believe it is safest to write about literature by men. The bulk of my reading and literary analysis has been of poetry, fiction and philosophy by men. To focus on women writers might mean more work than my time, money, and institutional support will allow.

I can, however, investigate male literature in a way that will help me and other women writers. Yes, I can examine images of creation in Whitman, Pound, Eliot, Williams, perhaps Stevens. I'll be a detective in the land of Eros, a spy in the house of Ed. I will explore, analyze, and report on the masculine creative drive, and the roles of the masculine and feminine principles, so we'll all see what's being put, thrust, read, written into us.

On the other hand, my real desire is to explore women's poetry, or at least one woman poet. *Maybe that one woman poet is really myself. Or my mother. My mothers. My sisters. And why am I writing this dry, disconnected, argumentative prose? Whose voice is this, anyway?* I want to make the personal, academic, and political leap into the field of feminist poetics: to see how women poets are creating *as women*.

I tell my dissertation advisor, Lillian Feder—the only woman on the faculty specializing in Modern Poetry—that I want to write on feminist poetics. I wrote my honor's and master's theses on Adrienne Rich's poetry when I was a student at City College, and want now to continue my work. Dr. Feder replies, "I am a living example of a feminist, yet I have no need to go about discussing it!" She then says, "prove it to me...prove that there is a need for this study...but don't use the word *feminist*."

Dirty word. How to get around it? If a woman is a poet and feminist, what is it that she would want to do? *Feminize form*. And if I don't want to prove something, if I don't want to argue and attack, what is it I must do? *Go into yourself. Search for the reason that bids you write.*

≈

I feared my mother. I have a vague recollection of sleeping with a knife under my pillow in case she came in during the night to give me a beating. I may not have actually kept the knife there, but it did, at least, become part of my imagination.

There were times when I knew a beating was coming, and if I had the strength of mind and courage, I would write a poem and slip it to my mother before she went into her fury. It never failed: it got me out of a beating.

Poetry helped me to stay connected to my mother, my body, myself, but this connection was maintained by a negative, polarized energy: approach-avoidance: connect, yes, but don't connect, stay back, protected. Expressions of love were permitted through poetry, but always with defense as the motive.

Poetry, with its ambiguity and easily accessed symbolism, was a convenient mask. Once my mother found my sister Adrienne's diary, in which she had written, "I hate my mother." My sister was beaten for writing those words, and I learned immediately and profoundly not to write honestly or openly; to disguise my feelings.

A childhood poem, "The Storm," begins:

> Here comes the storm, here comes the storm
> I see it in the hills
> He thunders, twirls and cracks and whirls
> And everything he kills

I was aware while writing the poem that the storm was a metaphor for my mother. I surrendered to her power, which became my own—violent, self-destructive. I also knew that disguising the truth in a figure of speech would enable me to express devastation and despair while protecting me from her further violence if I were to write honestly and she were to find the poem. Language, poetic devices, my thinking process itself—all became conspirators in the construction of denial, which continued to build, layer upon layer, throughout my writing life.

Now as an adult I understand that I perceived my mother's power as masculine in origin—I used the pronoun "he" to personify the storm, and have since learned that male physicians and psychiatrists had put her on the drugs to begin with. Some became her lovers. I eventually came to see my mother as a vehicle through which patriarchal power was transformed in the guise of maternal abuse on to me.

My identification with my father reinforced my denial and distance. In my eyes, he was strong, intelligent, made money, was out there in the world, arguing in court, getting awards. I learned through him the power of language, not in the form of poetry, but in manipulative argumentation and rhetoric. "First of all, second of all..." he would precede his reasons for things. I transcribed dictaphone tapes in his office, allowing his voice to flow through my senses and out through my fingers. I also took dictation through stenography, filed his papers away, typed, edited, proofread. Sometimes I appeared in court in his place to postpone trials.

It never occurred to me to enter the profession of law, as I detested the rhetoric and dry details, but I felt secure knowing that I could support myself typing: between my language skills and manual dexterity developed through piano playing, I could type over 100 words a minute nearly perfectly.

I communicated well with my father, intellectually. It became a way to stay connected to people safely, rationally, sanely. My father became a model for me of control. He was good at it. Though things seemed to always be falling apart, he always came to the rescue, was able to create a facade of control: over life, over others. Over me. But I could always outwit him. I used to write poetry while employed in his office, sneaking the writing in around my paid duties as a secretary:

> Oh Father, dear Father,
> I have used your xerox machine.
> Not for Law, or Biaggi, or Nixon,
> not even for the Boy Scouts.
> But for Art and Me.
> Will you pull the plug?

The thread I need to trace is the one I have constructed: the poet who used language to conceal and reveal, a palimpsest; to connect and hold back. The writer who is also a woman who perceived power and destruction as masculine in origin, a "he," a "storm," moving through the female form—be it my mother, my dissertation advisor, or—as I would later discover in my research—the passive female principle in art and philosophy which is associated with matter, formed in response to the active male principle.

November, 1977

How do I prove to Dr. Feder that this study is needed? I feel like a goddamned lawyer, trying to prove my client's innocence. Okay, start with Aristotle. He believed that female menstrual flow supplied procreative matter while the male semen provided spirit, movement, and form. This corresponds to his notion that "Vital Heat is included in semen," that "it is the natural principle in the spirit and is analogous to that element in the stars." Certainly, things must have changed. We all know that it takes an egg and a sperm; even science and physics would admit to relativity, the inseparability of energy and matter. Can a procreative metaphor be that much more powerful than the reality of it all?

"The brain," said Ezra Pound, is a "great clot of genital fluid...the phallus or spermatozoid charging, head-on, into the female chaos...Even oneself has felt it, driving any new idea into the great passive vulva of London."

This is almost funny. But it's merely a sexual metaphor that articulates Pound's conception of originality, only one poet's vision, anyway. But listen to this: George Dekker, speaking of Pound's Canto 47, notes that "a masculine principle (the sculptor, the ploughman), works *with* the feminine principle (the mountain, Tellus)...The sculptor transfers his love from a goddess, the woman, or the saint, to the stone, which because of the identity shared with the feminine principle, 'knows the form' which the lover-sculptor wishes to impart. The stone cooperates, as the woman cooperates in the sexual act...she yearns for the form which the male alone can give her."

She yearns for the form which the male alone can give her?

≈

Carl Jung, in his search for a mythical basis of reality, longed for the "former image of matter—the Great Mother," and he was disturbed that "what was the spirit is now identified with intellect and thus ceases to be the Father of All." Herbert Read, using Jungian terminology to discuss *The Origin of Form in Art*, assumes that the gender of the poet is male by the very terms he employs. He identifies the muse solely with the *anima*, a female archetype found in the male gender, and asserts that "it is very difficult for a man to distinguish himself from the anima, but that seems to be precisely what the poet does in the act of composition."

≈

The assumptions and associations reside more deeply and powerfully in the human psyche, I believe, than any individual set of biographical factors. Personal history like my own may account for some of the debilitating tension for women poets; but it cannot explain its prevalence and universality, nor help to change it at the core.

〰️

"Eroticism is *exciting*," Shulamith Firestone insists in *The Dialectic of Sex: The Case for Feminist Revolution*. "No one wants to get rid of it. Life would be a drab and routine affair without at least that spark...When we demand the elimination of eroticism, we mean not the elimination of sexual joy and excitement but its rediffusion over...the spectrum of our lives." Of course, *rediffusion*, good word. How else to transform the binary patterns?

But the situation, according to Dorothy Dinnerstein, is bleak, urgent. She opens her book, *The Mermaid and the Minatour: Sexual Arrangements and Human Malaise* with the vision of human extinction resulting from "our prevailing male-female arrangements...a massive communal self-deception, designed to allay immediate discomfort and in the long run—a run whose end we are now approaching—suicidal."

Oops. Not only am I sliding into some kind of apocalyptic vision, but I am beginning to distrust intimacy and sexuality; I am also taking major detours into areas of study and scholarship that appear to have little relevance to literature. But wait a minute, even Feder, in her seminar "Myth in Modern Poetry," described all poetry as "the eternal struggle between Eros and Thanatos."

〰️

I will name the female erotic imagination *Eras*.

Lindenhurst, November 14, 1981

I'm reading Susan Griffin's *Pornography and Silence*: "pornography is an expression not of human erotic feeling and desire, and not of a love of the life of the body, but a fear of bodily knowledge, and a desire to silence eros."

Is this silenced eros really eras? Griffin continues:

> As we explore the images from the pornographer's mind we will...see that the bodies of women in pornography, mastered, bound, silenced beaten, and even murdered, are symbols for natural feeling and the power of nature, which the pornographic mind hates and fears. And above all, we will come to see that "the woman" in pornography, like "the Jew" in anti-Semitism and "the black" in racism, is simply a lost part of the soul, that region of being the pornographic or the racist mind would forget and deny. And finally, we shall see that to have knowledge of this forbidden part of the soul is to have eros.

To reclaim the soul is to reclaim eros? Yes, for women poets to feminize form, we must reclaim eros, which in the process of re-claiming becomes *eras*. Have I been a "spy in the house of Ed," like Anais Nin, "a spy in the house of Love?" Where is the forbidden part of my own soul? When did I lose it?

〜〜

I need to understand the writer-student-poet in myself who was taught to distrust her own inner space, power and sexuality; who has used analysis for security, to find answers. Who internalized patriarchal thought. Between the security of analysis I found in my connection with my father, the family violence channeled through my mother, and the kinds of signals and directions of the academic world, I found it much safer, practical, and just plain wise to work intellectually while subversively identifying as the poet; and to act out traditional gender roles of daughter, student and wife while naming the authentic part of myself a "spy."

When I had to choose between "literature" and "creative writing" for an undergraduate major, I figured, why not go with "literature," why not go ahead and argue a thesis? As I continued to engage in intense literary analysis, writing became my enemy: disembodied, abstract, dry. There was an intellectual posture and tone that seemed to be required in graduate work, exacerbated by the polarized vocabulary used to describe the fields of study, *Creative Writing* and *Literature*. If the only forms deemed "creative" were poetry, fiction and drama, then was the rest of my writing *not creative*?

〜〜

I am reading Elizabeth Janeway's "Who is Sylvia? On the Loss of Sexual Paradigms." The theory is heavy, the abstractions intense, yet it is reinforcing something in my gut, something I perceived a couple of years ago in my writing on Plath:

> We have to invent not only new paradigms but new selves, selves capable of working out the significant generalizations that will make our existence coherent and structure our purposes...Any polarity is dangerous to creative thought. Thesis and antithesis claim to sum up the world and resolve our puzzles by merging into a synthesis, but what, we should ask, has got left out because it did not figure in either thesis or antithesis?

Now pulled in two directions—"investigating" the literature of men or "exploring" the poetry of women—why not take the safe route? Why not continue the role of a spy in the house of Ed?

Because something is changing. Something is happening in feminism, in the academic world, in criticism, in poetry, in me.

The Death of a Beautiful Woman

...is the most poetical topic in the world
Edgar Alan Poe

Rego Park, March 15, 1978

My dissertation prospectus has been accepted. I titled it *The Feminization of Form: A Study of the Creative Process in the Poetry of Plath, Sexton, Levertov and Rich*. I was lucky, and am reassured. One of the professors on the dissertation committee commented on the acceptance form that it was very well written. He is the same one I met with yesterday, to discuss my oral exams. He is a Medievalist. First he acknowledged reading the prospectus. Then he told me: "you're not going to find any of *that* in the Middle Ages."

I let the remark slide. His attitude pisses me off, but I need to stay quiet. I need to know what to study for the Orals. I've been advised that the procedure is to select two examiners for each of the three historical periods you choose to be examined on, and then to work out with each professor a list of agreed upon texts and topics. For a minor in Medieval Literature, I'm asking him and another Medievalist, Martin Stevens, whom I haven't met yet.

"What am I responsible for?...which texts?" I asked.

"Everything. Everything." He waved his arm, dismissing me, then escorted me out of his office.

November 16, 1978

I'm pregnant. I wrote a letter to the English Department requesting a leave of absence. I guess I'll work on the feminization of form on my own. Maybe I'm better off this way, working outside the institution. Isn't that what Adrienne said? *The institutional will fuck you up...*

January 2, 1979

When is the baby supposed to start kicking?

Sid Feshbach, my old Honors mentor, sent me an essay on H.D.'s poetry. He's still sending me articles, books, on women's poetry, on poetics. It's been lovely having this time to lay back and read.

And to still have Sid's support. He was the one who suggested I read Adrienne Rich when he was my mentor at City College. He said that she would be a visiting professor the semester that I would be writing my honor's paper. He gave me her phone number, urging me to call. At first I was annoyed and resistant, believing I'd been shoved into feminism because I was a woman. And imagine calling someone like Adrienne Rich, out of the blue!

But it worked out. I once told Sid that he was like a "father" that planted the "seed" and sent me to Adri... He quickly interrupted me, clearly uncomfortable with the analogy.

April 5, 1979

I'm reading Elaine Showalter's "Feminist Criticism in the Wilderness." It seems that I haven't been alone in my tug of war between "investigating" male poetry and "exploring" poetry by women. Showalter defines two modes of feminist criticism as the *feminist critique* and *gynocriticism*, the first "concerned with the feminist as *reader*, and it offers feminist readings of texts which consider the images and stereotypes of women in literature, the omissions and misconceptions about women in criticism, and woman-assign in semiotic systems." Gyno-criticism, on the other hand, is concerned with "women as *writers*—and its subjects are the history, style, themes, genres and structures of writing by women."

So my dissertation was to be either a "feminist critique" of male poets, or "gynocentric" and concern itself with woman-as-poet. I'm still not comfortable with this choice. What about the areas of overlap? Why either/or?

And since I have finally decided to write about women poets, it looks like I am moving in current critical directions. According to Showalter, "In the past decade...this process of defining the feminine has started to take place. Feminist Criticism has gradually shifted its center from revisionary readings to a sustained investigation of literature by women."

My decision, then, isn't really an "either/or"—male or female—one; rather, it is a process of first revising the male, and then (or simultaneously?) defining the female. I am confused. Is this a temporal process? Or is it one of dialectical synthesis effected through juxtaposition of opposing perceptions?

Just what does Showalter mean by "shifted its *center* from revisionary readings to a sustained investigation?" Is there a center? Does she mean focus? If so, is the process: focus on the male, shift the focus to the female, back and forth recursively?

It sounds very much like the dynamics and struggles of intimacy. Do we want to change the nature or behavior of the men in our lives? How do we deal with our attraction to (fear of?) male power—while finding and using our own? Must we define ourselves as women—apart from men? By connecting with other women, other women's language and sexuality? Is homosexuality, or at least homoeroticism, the answer?

It also occurs to me that if women writers have been perceiving and writing about patriarchal thought, language, and esthetics, then they might be writing out of and thus duplicating the male consciousness. How much have I and other women writers, trained in a patriarchal way of thinking and writing, internalized, assimilated, re-produced? How much have we appropriated a disembodied voice to serve the patriarchal institution of language?

Are we our own enemies, spies in our own homes, our own bodies? The bitterness, the anger, the fear: how much is directed against ourselves?

I must look at my own journey. I, too, years before reading Showalter, had shifted my perspective from the poetry of men to that of women, and had found that this "shifting" process was evident in the poetry of women, individually and collectively. This is central to what I call *the feminization of form: a shift in movement from internalization, assimilation and mimesis of a male perception to an organic rooting in female poetic identity and its formalization in language*. Movement: not through linear time or space; not through juxtaposition; but by *shifting*.

The notions of organic shifting and rooting help me to feel centered in an odd new way.

Lindenhurst, March 1980

Karen is eight months old. I'm exhausted, too tired to write. Need sleep. When will she sleep through the night? Need help. Sid sent me a gift subscription to *The American Poetry Review*, and I found the March/April edition mixed in with all the junk mail. There's an interview of Audre Lorde; something she says I must underline, put safely away, remember to bring it back into my writing, my life. Don't lose it. Karen's crying, I'm underlining: "The true feminist deals out of a lesbian consciousness whether or not she ever sleeps with women...the lesbian consciousness is an absolute recognition of the erotic within our lives and, taking that a step further, dealing with the erotic not only in sexual terms."

The lost part of the soul, Eras.

Rego Park, January 1978

I'll focus on women poets for my dissertation, and begin with Sexton and Plath. They epitomize the struggle of women poets who have internalized and absorbed male power to the point of self effacement.

In Sexton's poem, "The Love Plant," her lover's "freak but moist life-giving flower" "took root" inside her, only to "crowd me out/to explode inside me." Hoping to abort the form oppressing her, she tries in vain to "force it away"; but it "enlarges" and "thrives...on liquid solution." The substance, or "greenery hisses on."

Helplessly, she absorbs and nurtures the plant as it enters the "nasal passages...and thus to the brain" where it is at last externalized: "spurting out of my eyes." She becomes "inhuman...part of the green world," a "pink doll with her frantic green stuffing." This green world, as "Words for Dr. Y" reveals, is a place of "dead girls," a "sisterhood," a world ruled by a masculine power. He is the creative source—whether the product be the child, nature, or language—and victimizes whatever female form she can produce:

> Words waiting, angry, masculine,
> with their fists in a knot,
> Words right now, alive in the head,
> heavy and pressing as in a crowd.
>
> ...
>
> One we would surely overlook.
> So easily lost, a dead bee.
> So vulnerable.
> She is already trampled, that one.

In "The Twelve-Thousand Day Honeymoon," Sexton depicts the desolation of the female body in mythic imagery. Like Leda, she keeps "remembering, remembering/where the god had been/as he beat his furious wings," while her "vagina, where a daisy rooted,/where a river of sperm rushed home," lies "like a clumsy, unused puppet." The male erotic imagination—a river of sperm—moves through a passive female sexual channel.

Sylvia Plath also depicted the godhead in her poetry as male and destructive: a linguistically defined "he," within whose "volts" she "sizzled":

"By the roots of my hair some god got hold of me/I sizzled in his blue volts like a desert prophet."

The consequences? Disconnection from authentic female sensibility and form. How sad is the image of a mother detaching from her infant daughter in "Three Women":

> I see her in my sleep, my red terrible girl.
> She is crying through the glass that separates us...
> Her cries are hooks that catch and grate...
>
>   I leave someone
> Who would adhere to me: I undo her fingers
>   like bandages ...

September 1996, National Women's Studies Association Conference, Skidmore College, Saratoga, New York

Sylvia Plath's long dramatic poem, "Three Women," begins with an allusion to the story of Leda and the swan, the poet speaking of "the great swan, with his terrible look/Coming at me...from the top of a river." From this initial recollection of conception, the poem re-enacts the creative process as it moves from unconscious mythic experience to its formalization, symbolized by the birth of the children.

Each birth signifies one aspect of the nature of form: masculine in the first voice, (the "earth-mother") who bears a son, and the only one of the three who bears, keeps, and bonds with her child); disease, violence and death in the second voice (the "secretary" who miscarries, who conceives of form but can not bring it to fruition); and detachment from female identity in the third voice (the "student" who abandons and forgets her infant daughter).

The first voice's role in the creative process is ritualistic assimilation. She turns like the earth while leaves and petals attend her. The "sun and stars" regard her with attention, while a pheasant stands on the hill, arranging his brown feathers. The pheasant and the universal "sun and stars" are distinct from, and more powerful than, the personally female (moon), who merely "passes and repasses," as passively "astonished at fertility" as the woman herself, who "cannot help smiling" at what it is she "knows," or conceives. Soon she becomes "dumb and brown...a seed about to break." "The brownness is my dead self," she declares, and "it is sullen/It does not wish to be more, or different." Upon the birth of her son, she observes, "He is turning to me like a blind, bright plant/One cry. It is the hook I hang on to/and I am a river of milk."

The second voice's function is to translate perception. When she first sees the "small red seep" that signals a miscarriage, she blames it on men: "I watched the men walk about me in the office. They were so flat...now I had caught it/That flat, flat, flatness from which ideas, destructions, white chambers of shrieks proceed." She works as a secretary, seeing herself as a vehicle through which language is transmitted from men, and claims to "loose a dimension" while the "letters proceed from these black keys." She is unable to maintain a conception, becoming "flattened" or "voiceless."

She tries to restitch her identity when she returns home. "I wait and ache. I think I have been healing...My hands/Can stitch lace neatly on to this material. My husband/Can turn the pages of a book." She says that she and her husband can be "at home together" in a modern consciousness wherein it is merely "history" and "culture" that weighs oppressively upon her hands. If she can pull her focus off of the male perception and on to her own business of "healing," possibilities of what she imagines to be "tenderness" and "hope" will emerge. All the woman writer need do, as "stitcher" of new contextual material, is keep her eyes on herself while re-vising, re-forming, changing her negative perceptions.

This second voice was hampered, however, working with two other voices: The first voice kept assimilating and reproducing the male principle to the exclusion of the female. As a result, the third voice, a student who has learned to "re-member" or "imitate" the history of ideas, continues to detach from herself. "I remember the minute when I knew for sure," she begins,

> I remember a white, cold wing
> And the great swan, with his terrible look,
> Coming at me from the top of a river.
> He glided by; his eye had a black meaning.
> I saw the world in it—
> Every little word hooked to every little word, and act to act.
> I wasn't ready...I thought I could deny the consequence—

The profound detachment that permeates this poem is a result of the woman's "not being ready," despite apparent ritual, from the moment of conception—a linguistic rape of the woman's imagination. Her power was insufficiently developed to match the strength of the masculine creative mind—be it the swan, the men in the office, or, as the third voice puts it "the doctors/who move among us as if our bigness/frightened the mind." Internalizing male fear of her reproductive power, she turns with rage upon herself and her unborn child: "I should have murdered this," she says, "that murders me."

After the birth, she abandons her daughter:

> I see her in my sleep, my red terrible girl.
> She is crying through the glass that separates us...
> Her cries are hooks that catch and grate...
>
> ...I leave someone
> Who would adhere to me: I undo her fingers
>   like bandages

While the cries of the son were "hooks" that the first voice would "hang on to," the cries of the daughter are "hooks that catch and grate," irritants to be resisted, ignored.

In the closing passage, associations of the daughter are reduced to mere "lack" and "sorrow":

> I am solitary as grass. What is it I miss?
> The swans are gone. Still the river
> Remembers how white they were.
> It strives after them with its lights.
> ...finds their shapes in a cloud.
> What is that bird that cries
> With such sorrow in its voice?

The longing and sorrow are for that part of the self left out of the creative process, which we, the readers, may perceive as the "bird that cries," similar to the daughter crying through the glass. But the mother can't identify this voice of sorrow with her abandoned daughter. Vague meaningless dream shifts to mere absence, which she associates with the absence of the "swans," or the male principle, and immediately her imagination conjures up specific images and forms: The "river/remembers how white they were," and "it strives after them with its lights," finding their "shapes in a cloud." Attracted once more to the male principle, she "strives after it," continuing to assimilate, re-member, and reproduce its form.

The image of the "bird that cries/With such sorrow in its voice" is a result of a polarized consciousness that favors male power: it resists the alienated female principle, or "daughter" crying through the glass; in so doing it enables the conception of the "son," formed by the woman's memory of the male principle. The alienated female principle, or as Plath elsewhere in her poetry describes her, "the heroine of the periphery," tries desperately to enter the language and forms of patriarchy, but in the attempt, defines herself as partially formed, fragmented, stitched up, outlined in ghostly sketches. Images of the body that surface throughout this poem include heads, eyes, hands, mouths, blank faces, fingers and feet: ironically peripheral and segmental for a poem about the organic experience of childbirth.

By embracing and articulating the chaotic, associative, terrifying forms in her unconscious, and by rendering these forms from the perspective of a woman attempting to birth herself through them, Sylvia Plath gave to feminist poetic tradition an understanding of the need and nature of resistance, along with the urgency of connecting to positive, feminist support.

Rego Park, February 1978

I have come upon a remark by Edgar Alan Poe: "The death...of a beautiful woman is, unquestionably, the most poetical topic in the world—and equally it is beyond doubt that the lips best suited for such topic are those of a bereaved lover."

♒

Child: *Poe-Poet! Poet-Poe!* Isn't that the same person who wrote "The Bells?"

Scholar: Yes. People can write poetry and literary analysis.

Poet: I find that very difficult.

Child: But why does the beautiful woman have to die?

Scholar: It's only one voice. It's only one poet. Don't take it personally.

Child: That doesn't answer my question. Why does she have to die?

Woman: Because your mother died. She was beautiful. She used to write, remember? But she stopped. She went crazy.

Poet: Who is that speaking?

Scholar: I don't know!

Child: It's not fair. She shouldn't have to die. Or be stuck in a book. And why is the poet her lover?

Poet: I don't want to be her lover. I want one of my own.

Scholar: Hush. I'm trying to find answers.

Child: Do you find the answers in school?

Poet: There are no answers. But don't worry, I won't stop writing.

Scholar: Don't worry, I won't stop asking questions. I'll find answers.

Poet: Didn't you hear me? Questions don't have answers. Who are you trying to kid?

Woman: Where is my daughter?

Child: I want to play the piano.

Scholar: Go ahead. I'll figure something out.

Poet: Go ahead. I'll figure something out.

The Madwoman in the Attic

> *...women writers must kill the aesthetic ideal through which they themselves have been "killed" into art. And similarly, all women writers must kill the angel's necessary opposite and double, the "monster" in the house, whose Medusa-face also kills female creativity. For us as feminist critics, however, the Woolfian act of "killing" both angels and monsters must here begin with an understanding of the nature and origin of these images. At this point in our construction of a feminist poetics, then, we must really dissect in order to murder.*
>
>   Gilbert and Gubar

Lindenhurst, April 1997

My mother gave my sisters and me our middle names several years after we were born. Adrienne *Beth*, Patricia *Jane*, and Denise *Gale*. Since my middle name was never recorded on my birth certificate, I considered *Jane* to be unauthentic. I never liked it, never used it, and never identified myself with Jane (although she wore a nice red coat in my first grade reader, *Dick and Jane*). As I grew older, I reflected that since these were names my mother gave to us once she got to know us, they may say more about who we are than the names we were born into—at least who we are in our mother's eyes.

Twenty years ago, soon after my father died, I found an old leather volume of *Jane Eyre* in the attic while cleaning out the house. Inscribed on the inside cover was my mother's name, *Lillian Bellin*. I asked her if she remembered the book; yes, she did, it was her favorite novel. And yes, she named me Jane after Jane Eyre.

Did my mother perceive me as the dark, lost, passionate, persistent Jane to whom I would later so much relate? How much is my nature; how much did my mother either pass down to me or project on to me? How much of herself did my mother see—and fear—in me, and how much of that fear did I internalize?

"Little Lily" they called me when I was born because I looked so much like my mother. And, my mother told me, I was beautiful; she would dress me in bonnets and people would stop and stare. I detested the resemblance. I didn't want to be like my mother: beautiful and trapped: addicted to drugs, sex and men: suicidal, violent, insane.

It was the madwoman in the attic—Bertha—I feared. In my mother, myself, my fate.

〰

I sensed, even as a child, that a personal mythology was active in my life, as there was in Jane Eyre's. Names, especially, gave me clues. My father, the lawyer, the law-giver was named Moses. My mother, the child-abuser, the estranged, was named Lillian—the beautiful but fickle Lily, the outraged Lilith. I was the daughter of Moses and Lilith, a frustrating blend of patriarchal law and angry, alienated womanhood.

The two poets I read during graduate school *for myself*—deeply and wholly as a woman and as a poet—were named Adrienne (Rich) and Denise (Levertov), the names of my own sisters. My full first name, Patricia, I understood as the feminized form of a classical Roman noble figure: a patrician. My father's family name, Falk, is rooted in the falcon, bird-bard of prey; my mother's maiden name, Bellin, contained the *bell*.

Hear the ringing of the belles bells belles bells belles.

〰

Up in the attic, packed in the same box as *Jane Eyre*, was a copy of D.H. Lawrence's, *Lady Chatterley's Lover*. I had first discovered it when I was a child, hidden under the towels in the linen closet outside my parents' bedroom. I would take the novel downstairs into my own bedroom, reading chapter after chapter over several days, but always sliding it under the towels by early morning. I am re-reading it now, startled at the mention of Jane, partner to John Thomas. I had been about eight years old when I first read:

> The man looked down in silence at his tense phallus. "Ay!" he said at last, in a little voice. "Ay ma lad! Tha'rt theer right enough. Yi, tha mun rear thy head! Theer on thy own, eh? an' ta'es no count o' nob'dy! Tha ma'es nowt o' me, John Thomas. Art boss? of me? Eh well, tha'rt more cocky than me, an' tha says less. John Thomas! Dost want *her*? Dost want my Lady Jane? Tha's dipped me in again, tha hast. Ay, an' tha comes up smilin'.—Ax 'er then! Ax Lady Jane! Say: Lift up your heads o' ye gates, that the king of glory may come in. Ay, th' cheek on thee! Cunt, that's what tha'rt after. Tell Lady Jane tha wants cunt. John Thomas, an' th' cunt o' Lady Jane!

I must have had difficulty, as a child, reading through the thick dialect, but I'm sure I figured out that John and Jane were names for sexual organs, and that Jane was somehow related to "cunt," functioning like a "gate" through which John's "glory" might proceed.

Amityville, October, 2003

I've been researching the history of *Jane*. She seems to function as locus and gatekeeper of female sexuality, a natural, secular, unified source of women's power. But when transfigured into patriarchal form, she's split into the kinds of polarities embodied in the Roman god Janus, the mythic gate-keeper. He stands at the gate with two faces in opposite directions: one for coming and one for going; one for beginning and one for ending; one for looking one way, one for looking another. At times of war, the gate is open; in times of peace, closed. Unfortunately, the only times of commerce between public and private spheres are those of violence; peace trapped within the confines of the gates. This concept says something about the escalation of violence in systems of thought, in forms of relationships, and in institutions of government structured on models of polarity.

Despite this deeply rooted myth of masculinity, power and polarity, Jane has evolved into an image of "everywoman," fighting for control over her own gate and gate-keeping. Yeats, for example, based his series of Crazy Jane poems on a homeless woman named Mary; I've always seen Yeats' *Jane* as an unconventional, aging, outspoken, nearly mad hag. She's often isolated and disappointed in love: While "Naked I lay/The grass my bed," she becomes "a road/That men pass over." Still, she refuses to be silenced: "my body makes no moan/But sings on."

November 2, 2003

Last week I emailed Patricia Monaghan, asking her what she knows of the relationship of *Crazy Jane* to *Janus* and the Celtic *Janet*. She replied: "I used to live in Gort near the Yeats Tower. Supposedly [Crazy Jane] was a tinker (now traveler or itinerant) woman from near Loughrea who had many lovers and spurned the church...As for Janus, I've come up with the information that all Janus figures in Celtic lands are Romano-Celtic, with little Celtic and lots of Romano. An import, in other words." Patricia said she wasn't sure about the link to Janet, but a couple of days ago, I found the Tam Lin Ballad on line and sent it to her. Today she wrote back that of course, Janet was the earthy, human counterpart to the Sidhe:

Aha, TAM LIN! Now that helps. I had forgotten the name of the woman in the ballad. I'm going to write to a couple of Irish-speaking friends in Ulster to find out about the name. I know it as an Ulster name only, not Irish in general, so it would have made sense that it migrated via Scotland (where lived a similar figure, Thomas the Rhymer, who didn't alas have a Janet). I do know the figure who seduced Tam Lin, the leannan sidhe, the fairy lover. La Belle Dame Sans Merci...the leannan sidhe is the force that steals poets away from this world, so that they are never satisfied after she jilts them and returns them to the world. Here Janet seems an alternative to the soul-sapping sterile loveliness of the leannan sidhe. A real earth-bound breathing woman, not a vision of loveliness... I'm so interested in your connection of Janet and Jane and form. Loving this exchange!! PM

So Jane's roots are as much Celtic as Roman, and Celtic Janet passes on to Jane the qualities of an "earth-bound breathing" woman. Real. Authentic.

Here's the plot of the Tam Lin ballad: Tam Lin is a mortal man held in bondage by the Fairies and soon, on Halloween, he will be sacrificed to hell. Until then, he remains a hovering spirit guarding the Carterhaugh woods. Janet, the King's daughter, defies her father's orders that forbid maidens from entering the forest. Once there, she summons Tam Lin by plucking a rose, and later returns home pregnant. Again she defies her father, refusing to marry any of the men of the royal hall in order to give her child a name; she returns to the woods to gather herbs for an abortion. She also rescues Tam Lin from the Fairies and his hellish fate by hiding at the crossroads, pulling him from his horse, and holding on to him while he is transformed back into human form—naked and needing her protection.

Echoes of Charlotte Bronte's *Jane Eyre:* Jane sitting by the stile, soon to rescue Rochester, who falls off his horse, as well as Rochester's final condition of becoming stripped and blinded by the end of the novel while transformed by Jane's courage and compassion.

What had to wait until the 20th century, however, was Jane's insistence on taking control of her reproductive power—when she went underground as a political activist in the 1960's.

Lindenhurst, April 1997

Laura Kaplan, in *The Story of Jane: The Legendary Underground Feminist Abortion Service,* describes how the network provided safe, illegal abortions to women in Chicago in the 1960's. She tells how the network got its name:

> Late in the spring, they picked a name for their group: The Abortion Counseling Service of Women's Liberation. But they also needed a simpler code name. As they worried over the details of their work, Jenny said, "It looks like we're creating a monster." Lorraine answered, "Well in that case, I like my monsters to have sweet names, like Fluffy or Jane." Jane seemed a good choice. No one in the group was named Jane and Jane was an every woman's name—plain Jane, Jane Doe, Dick and Jane. The code name Jane would protect their identities while protecting the privacy of the women contacting them.

The Abortion Counseling Service may not have been aware of Janet's history, her knowledge of abortive agents, and her insistence on using them, but they certainly tapped into an important literary and political figure.

Jane is as powerful as a "monster" but has a "sweet" plain name. She's a code, a sexual code. She's hanging out with Dick.

She is authentic female power operating within patriarchy.

Because she is often invisible to the patriarchal eye, she can move around in "plain" sight. According to Kathleen Spivack, whose use of Jane as persona enabled her to write *The Jane Poems* (1974), a powerful sequence of political poetry, "Jane is Everywoman: she is a pilgrim through her times." She's simple, honest and open, but she has the potential for the kind of rage we see in Jane Eyre, who, when manipulated, trapped, and marginalized, projects her alter ego as Bertha, the madwoman in the attic.

Amityville, November 5, 2003

Found a couple of interesting websites on line. *Janemag.com* is the site for Jane Magazine, a periodical launched in 1997 by Jane Pratt. The magazine is aimed at young women who consider themselves outspoken and unconventional, a remnant, perhaps, of "Crazy Jane." There's also *Educatingjane.com*, described as "a national site for girls, their parents and educators dedicated to girls' self-esteem, self-awareness, and involvement in the world."

Good.

Lindenhurst, May 9, 1997

Jane has been the identity I've denied, the spirit buried, the vision and power distrusted. Yet she always seems to push her way into my writing. She won't be silenced, locked in an attic, or buried alive. She connects me to a matriarchal heritage, and whether I like it or not to my mother. Jane's power, projected at times as Bertha, has helped me to steal and salvage what I needed from my mother. A poem I wrote at about the age of 12:

> I found a china cup
> In an old trunk upstairs
> Delicate and petal-soft
> I handled it with care
>
> Little hearts and tiny bells
> Were painted on with love
> And when I turned it upside-down
> There sat a soft white dove
>
> It shimmered, sparkled,
> when it was turned
> to have this magic cup
> I yearned
>
> Carefully I wrapped it
> And carried it with me
> To bury it far in the earth
> Beneath a tall oak tree
>
> Next day found the attic burned
> All turned to ash and fog
> With all her old mementos gone
> I remember how my mother sobbed
>
> They said nothing could be saved
> So my plan had gone fine
> Since mother thought it had burned too
> The china cup was mine.

I wanted something from my mother: love, music, peace: the heart, the bells, and the dove. If I couldn't get it in real life, I could at least steal my own heritage, whatever genetic or mythical star that was passed on from her to me. I didn't want to kill the madwoman in the attic. Rather, I could save her from the fire (had I started it myself, like Bertha?). Instinctively, as a dog buries its bone, I buried the cup in the earth by a tree, a marker.

My mother found the poem lying around the house, and she wrote me one back, slipping it on to my bed. I don't remember the entire poem, though the opening phrase has stayed with me: "Do you really think..."

Lindenhurst, May, 1983

Went to the Graduate Center yesterday. I met with Jane Marcus, new to the English Department faculty, and told her I was re-enrolling in order to finish. I had read her essay, "Storming the Toolshed," and told her I liked the metaphor. Then, when I told her about the work I've been doing, she ran to the bookshelf and pulled out a book, *Stealing the Language: The Emergence of Women's Poetry in America*, by Alicia Ostriker. Jane said it's already been done. Too bad! "She's stolen your thunder, huh?"

I picked up my own copy in the bookstore and started reading while waiting for the train at Penn Station.

All the major developments in women's poetry are covered: rejection of a dualistic, polarized intellectualism, or "ogocentricity," in favor of a woman's centered perception, or "gynocentricity"; the impetus toward organic rooting in female identity through the creation of images of sexuality, reproduction, childbirth and motherhood; the poetics of rage; the reconstruction of the oppressor's language, consciousness, myth, and mythopoetic practice; making flesh into word.

Ostriker creates a continuous female poetic tradition in the context of mainstream history and culture, interweaving feminist poetics with a critical visionary eye. For this I am grateful. Because of her work, I can now approach the field of women's poetry and critical analysis from the perspective I have always wanted to take.

Tomorrow I am driving into the city. Jane Marcus invited me to a publisher's reception for Adrienne Rich at Lincoln Center. I wonder if Adrienne will recognize me.

August, 1995

My book of poetry, *In the Shape of a Woman*, has been published. I dreamed last night that I descended into the earth, searching for my cup. Time and the elements had destroyed it; the tree roots were still there, but the cup had disintegrated. Had patriarchy destroyed my cup? No, the cup is merely a symbol, and I have memory, and I have—yes, in my dining room is a breakfront full of beautiful, individual china teacups.

I sent my mother a copy of my book. She asked if I ever saved the poem I wrote about the cup. "Yes," I told her, "I saved it. Do you remember writing a response?"

"Yes," she replied. "Send me a copy of yours, maybe I'll write one again."

Maybe she will. My mother is in her seventies. She lives in Florida with her fourth husband, preferring to forget or to deny the past. We never talk about it. My feminist grounding, years of therapy, and maybe simply my own aging—have helped me to understand my mother's pain, and to separate from it; to understand that her choices were limited, her illness beyond her control.

Still, at times the rage returns.

1997

Crazy Jane

For too long I have carried you
inside me, color and substance
of lead, burden of darkness and dawn.

Now morning cracks the sky,
pulls clouds asunder
topples every unrelenting Oak.

Stones break open, render seed
scatter sow and spit out life.
It happens as I speak.

It happens as I thrust my hand
into my heart and demand
your blessing.

The Day the Music Died

Jamaica Estates, June 4, 1962

My sister Adrienne went to the prom last night looking beautiful. She wore a blue satin strapless gown, light blue heels—dyed to match the dress—and her hair was done in a French twist. I sat in the bathroom and watched as she painted on bluish-purple eye shadow and thick black eyeliner. Then pink blush above her high cheekbones, darker tones just under the bone.

I don't belong to this ridiculous world of women, despite the fact that my breasts are swelling and curls of pubic hair are thickening between my legs. I do feel the stirrings of desire, yes, in my body, my mind, and my heart, but that desire is satisfied only when I close myself off in my room, reading, writing, painting.

I still play the piano—though not often—and only when no one is home. It has begun to feel that when my fingers run across the keys, someone else is playing. I no longer take lessons. Mr. Breed, who helped me through Chopin and Beethoven, left a couple of years ago. He and my mother had been having an affair, and I guess the lessons ended along with their love.

I got really mad at Mr. Breed that last time, anyway. I had worked hard on *Moonlight Sonata*, had the first two movements down perfectly in one week. After I played it for him, he said, "your mother's been helping you with this, hasn't she?" He had a funny look in his eye, and then he turned and smiled at my mother, who was lying on the couch, listening, smoking, running her hand through her black hair. He gave her the credit! Damn him. Must I too have sex with him to get his approval?

∿∿
∿∿

My stomach isn't so good lately. When I first noticed the blood, my mother took me to Harvey, our family doctor. He has an office and an examining room attached to his house on Union Turnpike in Flushing—though most of the time when we are sick he comes to our house with his black bag and needles. He gives us shots, especially my mother, who needs demoral and morphine. He is always very nice to me, though my parents call him a "real nut." He seems to be often entangled in legal affairs, and my father is his lawyer. In my father's office, where I work sometimes, there is an entire file cabinet draw filled with files on Harvey's cases. He gets into trouble a lot.

On one of my parents' trips to Europe, they brought back a funny piece of sculpture—it's of a skinny man, twisted, in the costume of a surgeon who looks exactly like Harvey, cutting up a body. We laugh about it because it looks so much like him: wire-rimmed glasses, small beady eyes, sunken cheeks, and pointy nose. It sits on the living room shelf among all the other knick-knacks.

Harvey was the first doctor I saw for my stomach. He examined me inside with long metal instruments. When he said I had worms, I thought I would die of shame. Eventually, I was taken to cancer specialists in the city, and to my relief found out that it wasn't worms, it wasn't even cancer. I have something like ulcers—ulcerative colitis. It's hard to say those words. The doctors say I can't eat vegetables any longer, they are bad for my stomach.

Now my mother can't force me to eat them. She knows how much I hate them, and just to be mean, she sometimes puts only vegetables on my plate, making me eat them before I get any other food or water. My sisters get a full plate of food, and I watch them eat the mashed potatoes, roast beef—whatever the maid has cooked—and then I turn and stare at the cold broccoli or slimy green beans on my plate. Sometimes I bribe my sisters: if they eat my vegetables or go to the bathroom and flush them down the toilet, I'll become their slave for a day.

〰〰

My stomach's okay today, though it was beginning to act up last night when Adrienne left for the prom. Finally, I got to sleep. Then the door bell rang at two in the morning, and I awoke to a commotion in the foyer. I got out of bed and walked down the hall into the kitchen, where I could see into the front marble hallway. Three policemen were talking to my father. My mother was on the staircase, clinging to the banister, hysterical, screaming that something must have happened to Adrienne. But no, something was going on that had to do with Harvey. Since my father is his lawyer, the police wanted to talk to him about something awful Harvey has done. It seems that a girl went to Harvey to get an abortion. She died while he was working on her, and he must have gotten scared—it's against the law to do what he was doing. And right there, while she lay dead on the table, he cut her up with a saw, chopped her up into little pieces, and put the pieces of her body down the garbage disposal, grinding them up.

I get sick thinking about it, really sick.

〰〰

The story has been on TV and in all the newspapers. Her name is Barbara Jane Lofrumento and she was a college student. Harvey couldn't be found for weeks. Then, a few days ago, he contacted my father from Andorra, a tiny country in Europe near France. My mother and father went there amid a barrage of publicity to talk him into coming back to the United States—something called extradition.

They came back yesterday. My father asked me to make a scrapbook for him, and I will do as I am asked. He wants to save all the newspaper clippings, highlighting the important role he has taken. He wants me to cut and scotch tape all the pictures, including the ones where he and Harvey are outside the Supreme Court, standing on the top of the steps that lead down to the street.

I am good at cutting out articles, careful not to slice through a word or a column of print, taking extra care to leave a little space around the black and white photographs, to stay along the margins, the sharp edge. But sometimes I make a mistake, and the scissors slip over the line into the picture of Barbara Jane. It feels like I am cutting myself.

Amherst, July 17, 1996

Memories fade, become buried under layers of daily life, other events, passions, disasters, blessings: my parents' divorce in 1965; my marriage in 1971; my father's death in 1977; the birth of my daughter in 1979; the publication of my book and my divorce from Bob in 1995. But like a monster one believes has died but is merely asleep, stones break open, ghosts return.

I am walking and having a cigarette outside of Sid's house in Amherst. He and his wife Oriole live next door to Peter Elbow in a house on a cliff overlooking The University of Massachusetts. Sid is now helping Karen to pick a college and has set up an appointment for her with the dean at U. Mass this afternoon. Oriole and Sid have insisted we stay a few days in their home. Dear, dear Sid—my old mentor. How many hundreds of postcards he's sent me, how many letters have I sent him? Years without seeing him, but lots of letters and books and articles. Then, when Canio asked me to find someone to write an introduction to *Shape*, I asked Sid, who had retired from teaching and had moved from the city to Amherst. He had never read my poetry before, only my literary analysis and scholarship. But he read the manuscript and said he'd be happy to write an introduction.

Now Karen's looking at colleges in the Amherst area, and it has become a wonderful reason to see him and meet his wife Oriole.

I am smoking and walking, wondering if I'll run into Peter Elbow. I pick a wild flower from the field, thinking maybe I'll pick more and bring a small bouquet to Sid and Oriole. Or maybe I'll give it to Karen, who is confused and scared about finding the right college. I remember the flower I used to draw—actually doodle in class during tedious college lectures—a round circle for a center and long oval petals flowing outward from the circle. How thrilled I was when I noticed that Adrienne Rich had been drawing the same flower in her own doodles.

Suddenly, I sense danger, and for some reason, rather than take the wild flower with me, I put it on the windshield of my car, parked at cliff's edge. I return to Sid's house for breakfast. He and Oriole seem openly disturbed; they have something to show me. Harvey made the papers again, *The New York Sunday Times*. It's open to an article, complete with photographs, on the kitchen table.

Harvey had become a psychiatrist while serving his prison sentence and is now in practice, working for an upstate New York social services agency. It seems that he had abruptly taken a young woman off of anti-depressants; she then committed suicide. This prompted his dismissal along with criminal charges, leading to further investigation. The *Times* includes some photographs and text of the old story from 1962.

Lindenhurst, July 22, 1996

The crash of Flight 800 off the south shore of the island is all over the news. I had heard about it while I was up in Amherst at Sid's. When I got home, I put the *Times* article about Harvey in a drawer along with all the other old ones. My father's secretary Marie has given me copies of all the newspaper clippings she had kept after my father's death—in English and in French—that had been gathered, cut and pasted in 1962, tracking the coverage up through Harvey's trial.

My mother says that my father was so obsessively high on the wealth of publicity that Harvey believed he wasn't getting the best legal representation. So he took my father off the case and turned it over to a specialist in criminal law. Harvey was finally convicted of performing an "illegal operation" and improper disposal of a body. He couldn't be charged with murder since there was no body to be found—only a ring, a piece of tooth.

My parents threw out that awful piece of sculpture they had brought back from Europe.

Lindenhurst, 1997

Sculpture can get thrown out, but memories are another story. This monster has lived in my mind, body, imagination for 35 years. And I want it out.

In the imagination of the 12 year old girl, I was that woman. I had been on that same examination table, had been entered by that same man. And my father defended him. I worked for my father. I took a part. I learned how to cut, cut, and cut some more. I learned analysis. Annihilation. Disempowerment. Consequences of intimacy, sexuality, pregnancy: creativity.

The lost part of the soul, Eras.

Today Life Opened Inside Me

Rego Park, 1974

Heard on the news this morning that Anne Sexton killed herself. Then I packed up my book bag and caught the train to school, figuring I'd stop at Adrienne's office before class. She didn't look sad when I got there; she seemed furious but distant. She told me she was on her way to give a talk on Anne. Would I like to walk across campus with her?

♒

"Anne Sexton was a poet and a suicide." As Adrienne continues, my mind drifts: I have to be in court tomorrow to testify on behalf of my husband, Bob. I think of the violence, the cops. I hear Adrienne, "her head was often patriarchal, but in her blood and her bones, Anne Sexton knew." Knew. Knew what? We must not, Adrienne admonishes, be "content to produce intellectual or artistic work in which we imitate men"; we must "fight...in ourselves...the images patriarchy has held up to us."

I'm tired. I don't want to fight. Yes, I know that the images are powerful, but we have to go more deeply. Beyond the images. To the rhythms, the assumptions, the attitudes. We have to change the whole process.

Fight the images patriarchy has held up to us. How. They are, I think, more powerful than I.

The Graduate Center, CUNY, New York, December 1978

Am reading Yeats for Lillian Feder's Ancient Myth in Modern Poetry course. In *A Vision*, he imagines "the annunciation that founded Greece as made to Leda, remembering," he says, "that they showed in a Spartan temple, strung up to the roof as a holy relic, an unhatched egg of hers; and that from one of her eggs came Love and from the other War. But all things are from antithesis," he continues, "and when in my ignorance I try to imagine what older civilization that annunciation rejected I can but see bird and woman blotting out some corner of the Babylonian starlight."

Yes, for Yeats, as for all thinkers and writers for whom "all things are from antithesis," there will always be that "unhatched egg," perceived as a vague dream/woman/bird, some alienated female principle left out of the dialectic: from one egg came Love, from the other, War; there still remained the "unhatched egg." In the whole dualistic drama of Eros and Thanatos, an "unhatched egg."

Left out.

Well, what about Whitman? His is a "democratic" esthetic, biologically based in the "body electric," where we often enjoy images of strong, independent women, passages where the feminine principle seems to be the assertive, creative agent from which is issued language, humanity, self-concept:

> Unfolded out of the strong and arrogant woman I love, only
>   thence can appear the strong and arrogant man I love,
> Unfolded by the brawny embraces from the well-muscled woman
>   I love, only thence come the brawny embraces of the man,
> Unfolded out of the folds of the woman's brain come all the
>   folds of man's brain, duly obedient...
> First man is shaped in the woman, he can then be shaped in
>   himself...
> Unfolded out of the inimitable poems of woman come the poems
>   of man (only thence have my poems come)...

Because of the woman's self-directed power and its embodiment in form, this may be a good example of the feminization of form, at least from the male perspective. I notice, however, that the poems in which the woman is most powerful are the ones containing the least graphic sexual imagery. At times of the most explicit sexual imagery, *woman* in Whitman's poetry functions as a passage to the "greater" woman—the *Mother*—her value determined by her capacity and potential to produce offspring. When perceived as object of male sexuality, an entirely different, misogynist process unfolds:

> It is I, you women, I make my way,
> I am stern, acrid, large, undissuadable, but I love you,
> I do not hurt you any more than is necessary for you,
> I pour the stuff to start sons and daughters fit for these States,
> I press with slow rude muscle,
> I brace myself effectually, I listen to no entreaties,
> I dare not withdraw till I deposit what has so long accumulated
>   within me...

Kirkridge Retreat and Study Center, PA, May 1989

I step out of the car, stiff from the long drive; my eyes sweep over the vast fields and mountainous terrain, settling on an old, white, multi-winged farmhouse. My vision, however, is soon drawn to what appears to be a massive boulder far down the road, rising up out of an open, sloping meadow.

≋

Kirkridge is an old Celtic community in the mountains of Pennsylvania. I have been looking forward to this workshop for a long time: Denise Levertov's "Poetic Image as Spiritual Insight." Tonight, over dinner, I mentioned to Denise that I was working on a poem about entering a rock. Once inside, I begin to suffocate, terrified I won't find my way out.

"You might like that big stone structure on the far field," she responded. "Go through the cromlech and past the footbridge. There's an immense stone fortress, full of open spaces."

The cromlech is a mushroom-shaped portal, constructed of two huge upright boulders upon which rests another horizontal slab. Once through this portal, I descend along an incline; scattered to the right and left of the path are large stone figures in natural and human shapes.

After a few minutes I come to a round stone chapel. Inside it is dark and damp, a round, flat stone placed as a table in the center of the small space. There are candles and long wooden matches. I light a candle and think of my father, dead now 14 years. Back into the daylight and a short walk further on across the small foot-bridge that Denise has mentioned, I see more stone figures as well as a huge open stone "playhouse," where I can move in and out of the structure, freely.

The Graduate Center, CUNY, New York, 1984

Denise Levertov's concept of organic poetry is based on the belief that inherent in all experience, including that of the Self, is innate "form beyond forms" or "constellations" to be "apperceived" and translated by the poet through the "intuitive interplay of various mental and physical factors." So a woman-poet, as long as she "apperceives" her innate form and translates it through a process combining both "mental and physical factors," would be apperceiving, translating, and thus creating in art a form that is "feminized."

An examination, however, of some of her poetry reveals some important distinctions between what is apparently a "universal" (a linguistically defined male) esthetic and an organically female creative act.

> Blind to what he does not yet need
> He feels his way over broken glass
> to the one stone that fits his palm.
>
> When he opens his eyes he gives to what he gazes at
> the recognition no look ever before granted it.
> It becomes a word. Shuddering, it takes wing.
>
> from "Growth of a Poet"

The pronoun *he* is used in the universal sense, and the passage describes that aspect of "Organic Poetry" in which the poet intuits the unique, individualized form (the piece of glass). Then, upon "recognition" or "apperception" by the poet, the form (stone) metamorphosizes into language (word), and is finally released into consciousness, taking "wing."

There is a difference in tone, distance, movement, and sexual reference when Levertov speaks not *of* the poet but *as* the poet:

> The moon is a sow
> and grunts in my throat
> Her great shining shines through me
> so the mud of my hollow gleams
> and breaks in silver bubbles
>
> She is a sow
> and I a pig and a poet
>
> from "Song for Ishtar"
>
> When I am a woman—O, when I am
> a woman
> my wells of salt brim and brim
>   poems force the lock of my throat
>
> from "Cancion"

In both of these passages, the throat is an allusion to the poetic passage; in the first, the sow "grunts" in it; in the second, poems force the "lock" in it, enabling the poet to speak from an organic place of being.

The process of change in "Song for Ishtar" and "Cancion" is not the series of metamorphoses present in "Growth of a Poet." Rather, in "Song for Ishtar" a chain of identification is set up among Ishtar, moon, pig and poet, creating a passage for the "grunts" and "poems" to move through "the mud of my hollow" and break out through "the lock" of my throat" in "Cancion."

And in these poems, the poet is not described as "apperceiving" innate form and its metamorphoses, but passionately, subjectively, expressing in imagery suggestive of the birth process, the inspiration, translation, and release of poetic form. It is through this other—female inspired and female defined—process that the metamorphosis of *stone* into *word* and its release (taking wing) in "Growth of a Poet" can be accounted for.

Rego Park, April, 1979

I am big and round. The baby has started kicking. I love it. The cat likes to crawl on to my lap, and then she kneads her paws into my belly. There is a rhythm to her pressing and her purring. She knows something mysterious is going on inside me.

I am sure that the baby is a girl. I will name her Karen. Karen Anna.

Karen after Karen Schnitke. She played the piano in the school orchestra, was thin, pretty, talented, and she went out with that really cute guy, the artist. May my daughter never feel split between being a woman and an artist.

Karen after Karen in *Exodus*. May my daughter learn the meaning and courage of being a Jew.

And *Karen Anna* after Anna Karenina; reversed, inverted. May my daughter never know sexual shame nor condemnation.

And *Anna* in the center of her name, for the center of the sun, the centeredness I found reading Anne Sexton. May my daughter bear the fruits of Anne's poetic labor that Anne the woman-in-life would never enjoy.

Rego Park, June, 1979

I'm reading Anne Sexton. She knew she'd have to feminize the sources of creation were she to survive. Language, spirit, substance: all must embody the self-as-woman. Only when the myths are rewritten and God is redefined can authentic female identity and sexual power emerge.

In "Somewhere in Africa," the poet declares: "If this is death and God is necessary let him be hidden...Let God be some tribal female who is known...naked to the waist..." Once she finds "she of the origin, she of the primal crack, she of the boiling beginning" ("The Horoscope Poems, January 24") the poet can "bow my head to the meadow/the breast," and "raise my pelvis to God/so that it may know the truth of how/flowers smash through the long winter" ("The Fierceness of Female").

In touch with her origins, she channels that energy into form while affirming female life: "Today life opened inside me like an egg...there was the sun, her yolk moving feverishly." Internal and external symbols of life and power are female-defined: the egg, associated with fertility and reproduction; the sun, a traditionally masculine source of power, is linguistically marked as "she." Most important is the sense of concretion, the synthesis of matter and form.

Speaking of the sun, she says:

> I'd known she was a purifier
> But I hadn't thought
> she was solid
> hadn't known she was an answer.

"Live"

July 29, 1979

My daughter Karen Anna is born. She's a Leo, a sun sign.

A Life I Didn't Choose

> *A life I didn't choose*
> *chose me: even*
> *my tools are the wrong ones*
> *for what I have to do.*
>   Adrienne Rich

Rego Park, February, 1978

 My father has been dead for four months. A sudden heart attack. I had just turned 27 the month before and was an intern teaching my first class at Queensborough Community College.
 It was a remedial composition class. I was nervous at first, but because I was an intern, I was given a formula to follow. It's a five paragraph structure: an introduction leading to a thesis statement; three body paragraphs, each introduced by a topic sentence followed by details; a conclusion. The students were able to catch on quickly though they always seemed tired or bored.
 This semester I'm teaching a different course, a combined remedial and Freshman Composition class. Now I'm an adjunct at Kingsborough Community College. The campus is gorgeous, it even has a beach. But these students are restless, and the five paragraph formula is useless. Something's wrong. How will they ever get beyond five paragraphs later on?
 I've been reading up on writing pedagogy. Something is bothering me: here I am in front of all these students, supposedly to teach them how to write. How does my education in literature, Chaucer, philosophy, Latin, French, Italian, linguistics—how is it going to help me help them to write? There's a writer somewhere in me that wants to tell them, hey, just come out and say what you have to say. But they're frozen. They want to give me back something that they think I want.
 I want to do my own writing, dammit. Trying to write some poetry and to work on the dissertation prospectus. At the same time, I'm beginning to wonder about this tool called "language," sensing that conventional academic rhetoric might be working against me.
 There's also something about women's poetry that resists standard exegesis and analysis. I wish I had the freedom here at the Graduate Center that I did at City College. As an "honors" student, taking independent tu-

torials on the poetry of Adrienne Rich, I kept journals—hundreds of pages of reflective, exploratory writing. I never learned so much in my life.

Sid encouraged me. His fields are literary criticism and Joyce, so he's open to innovation, possibilities. I will always be grateful that he gave me the space to do what I wanted, to experiment and to challenge. And that's what I did in the Honors "Thesis": I wouldn't write a thesis, nope. I found that every thesis has a bloody antithesis that jumps right up and says, you're wrong dummy. Wanna fight?

It's that same polarization, creeping like a rat within the system of higher education.

So I explicated and re-explicated a few lines of a poem over and over again from multiple perspectives, ending up with over 100 pages of intensely focused analysis. I called my methodology "circular" and titled the paper "'Snapshots of a Daughter-in-Law:' Rich's New Rhetoric." Sid wrote a letter to the Honors Committee that would be evaluating my essay, explaining that it was "essentially unfinished" (and might never be), but that it ought to be passed on the basis of its innovation and the fact that I was learning so much.

I found that very cool.

When I expanded it into my master's thesis, I no longer had Sid to help me fight. The Committee insisted that I write a preface justifying my methodology. I did, got the MA, but wondered how much longer I could keep up this posture, this BS.

Soon after, I was interviewed by Allen Mandlebaum at CUNY's Graduate Center in what I had believed would be a *pro forma* meeting prior to acceptance into their Ph.D. program. I was coming in with honors, fellowships, straight A's and glowing recommendations.

I immediately realized that I was in enemy territory.

"What is your major field?"

"Modern Poetry."

"Oh. What was your Master's work on?" (*He knows all of this, dammit, he has all my records in front of him.*)

"The poetry of Adrienne Rich."

"Have you applied to any other graduate schools?"

"Just NYU."

"I suggest that you go there. You won't like it here."

Rego Park, June 1978

I should be reading more literary scholarship, but I am finding something important in composition theory. It seems that I'm not the only one finding myself working with Freshman Composition and Remedial English college students, wondering what I am doing here, and whether or not and how my rigorous intellectual and academic background can help. Previously labeled "creative" or "personal" forms of writing are becoming academically sanctioned. Peter Elbow, Marie Ponsot, Rosemary Dean, Dixi Goswami—a host of others—are talking about free writing, free association, clustering, use of poetry in the composition process, narration and description as viable, credible, even persuasive developmental methodologies for exposition. These forms of writing are being taught in the same rooms as philosophy and calculus, literary explication, linguistics.

What Susan Griffin and others have done in prose—written multi-layered exposition without the posture of a thesis subject to attack by an angry antithesis—has become an increasingly viable form of academic rhetoric.

The message: we can, and ought to, write from experience in addition to (or rather than?) responding to questions with what we believe might be the "right" answer which exists in the mind of the questioner. This is a pedagogical revelation, and coupled with my newly acquired sense of support from feminist writers and theorists, I begin to feel some sense of direction. If the path is not clear, defined, or familiar, and even if it is littered with old signs of danger, it is at least becoming directed.

What is clear: More and more teachers are finding ways to make education less isolating, more relaxed, truthful; to allow students to empower themselves in a global village increasingly complex, stressful, and mired with unauthentic rhetoric. Janet Emig defines this movement as the "tacit tradition." What the "cluster of scholars who make up the tacit tradition...share...is that, together, their work begins to provide research into writing...leading to the emergence of a new structure of ideas...a large change in thought really involves abandoning a paradigm...a whole way of thought."

≈

This is where feminist poetics and writing pedagogy are fused. Both movements, which have led to a reassessment of ways of knowing, are rooted in an understanding of the interpenetrating roles of intimacy and politics; both rely on organic paradigms rather than dualistic dogma; both insist on imaginative freedom and re-construction.

≈

Writing, learning, reading and teaching are acts of intimacy, not very different from the intimate relationships we have with art and the history of ideas; our own cultures; families, lovers, friends. And if I am struggling as a writer and a woman and a poet and a scholar with a dynamic of such a complicated and intimate nature, I will also need to work on—re-see, revise—multiple layers, levels, facets of being. I have a theory in my back pocket, that women poets can *feminize form*. But I need to be careful.

Susan Griffin: *When a theory is transformed into an ideology, it begins to destroy the self and self-knowledge*. Avoid ideology, reclaim myself, reclaim perhaps, my voice. Maybe someday help my students to re-claim their own.

Queensborough Community College, Bayside, New York, October, 1977

I sense a powerful voice in one of my students, Angelica, an Hispanic woman in her twenties, who really should be in an ESL class rather than remedial writing.

She has such a rich history, and such depth in her writing—at least in her journals. But there is nothing of herself in the flat five paragraph essay. She neatly repeats the question in a thesis, and point by point gives three examples as she is instructed. Then she labors over the grammar and spelling.

She's been giving me parts of her journals. We talked the other day in my office. Her real difficulty is not her inability to learn the language. She's working eight hours a day cleaning houses, caring for two young children, trying to appease her husband. He doesn't know she's taking classes at the college; she lies to him and says she's working in the evenings.

"What would happen if you told him?"

She looks away.

Rego Park, March 1975

I am living on the 11th floor of an apartment building across the street from Alexander's department store, overlooking the parking lot and the Long Island Expressway. Bob and I have been married four years, and during this time I've changed. I've grown away from him, doing what I need to do for myself. I struggle to hold on to our marriage and my sanity, but the more that I try to please him, to help him, the worse it all seems to get.

Rego Park, April, 1975

I'm in a program where I will complete my bachelor's and master's degrees at the same time, a BA/MA program. It's intense. I have about a year left to complete both degrees. Right how I'm taking 16 credits, half undergraduate, half graduate, while working on my honor's thesis on Adrienne Rich's poetry. Bob's also attending City College, and although he's keeping up his grades, he's also smoking weed and drinking heavily. The time I spend on my studies and writing has become a source of friction between us.

Last Tuesday I told Sid that I am considering withdrawing from the program. It's just too much. He said he didn't need to know the specific reasons, but has learned that they are usually personal. That night I sat out on the terrace for hours, thinking. I decided to stay in the program, to keep going.

Rego Park, June 1975

Today I received a letter from "Junction," a publication of Queens College. They want to publish my poem, "Rumble." My first publication! It begins, "listen   the sea can not be still." It ends, "a purple turgid denizen in its blue green lair/sometimes explodes and doesn't care."

Rego Park, 1978

I read my poems in public yesterday, for the first time. Someone from a woman's organization at the Graduate Center invited me to read with a few others. I hesitated, then said yes. The day before the reading, I went to a poetry reading at Womankind Books, a small bookshop and literary press in Huntington run by two lovely, openly gay women. After her reading, I spoke to the poet—I think her name is Lucille Clifton—and told her that the next day I would be giving my first reading and was really nervous. She put her huge hand around my upper arm and said, "honey, use that nervousness creatively!"

I'll never forget her words and the feel of her hand on my arm. I was nervous yesterday, but felt during the reading some incredibly warm and powerful energy coming through.

Lindenhurst, 1984

Have been auditing Rachel Brownstein's seminar at CUNY. Feminist Literary Criticism. It means leaving Karen with Tammy, the babysitter, driving to the station and parking, taking the train to the city, and then the subway up to 42nd Street and 6th Avenue. The seminar is only two hours long, but there's the traveling and research and reading and photocopy time: articles, books, pamphlets on reserve in the stacks. I'm overwhelmed with it all. Feminisms. Multiplicities. Factions. Arguments. Institutions.

I've become aware that my work on feminist poetry has been focused on white, privileged women poets. In my dissertation prospectus to the committee, I wrote that each poet—Plath, Sexton, Levertov and Rich—represented, in that order, one stage in a changing consciousness of women poets: the movement from internalization and mimesis of a patriarchal creative process to one organically female. Plath through resistance; Sexton, conscious change; Levertov through spiritual and organic grounding; Rich, radical feminism. I justified to myself that while these poets were all white and privileged, they were for just those reasons most likely to have assimilated and reproduced a white patriarchal esthetic, and therefore most important to look at as models of change.

But this is too narrow, simplistic. What about black feminism, lesbian feminism; then there's black lesbian feminism. Asian. Middle Eastern. Other social and cultural and linguistic and historical and philosophical...

Something important by Audre Lorde:

> When people of a group share an oppression, there are certain strengths that they build together. But there are also certain vulnerabilities. For instance, talking about racism to the women's movement results in "Huh, don't bother us with that. Look, we're all sisters, please don't rock the boat." Talking to the black community about sexism results in pretty much the same thing. You get a "Wait, wait...wait a minute: we're all black together. Don't rock the boat." In our work and in our living, we must recognize that difference is a reason for celebration and growth, rather than a reason for destruction...With respect to myself specifically, I feel that not to be open about any of the different people within my identity, particularly the 'mes' who are challenged by a status quo, is to invite myself and other women, by example, to live a lie. In other words, I would be giving in to a myth of sameness which I think can destroy us.

Touch it, be with it, don't fear it, connect. Leave space. Honor the space. Open the form. Connect not through sameness or difference but acceptance of *just that: space*. Several spaces. Celebrate and see what happens.

Why is it so hard to do that?

Skidmore College, Saratoga, New York, September 1996

I thought about Celeste yesterday, after many years. She was our "live-in maid," as we called her then—when I was a child. From 1955 through the early sixties, she took care of me: she gave me my bath, prepared my meals, and every morning before school, as I sat on the tall yellow chair by the kitchen stove, she brushed out my hair, twisting it into a ponytail with a thick colorful garter. I don't recall any real affection between us—Celeste's heart, I would learn, was with her own three children, living with their grandmother in Georgia. She had a son named Papa, the nickname given to him because he was the only male child of a fatherless family; yet the name of the man who fathered her children was Sonny. It was a great ironic twist. All of us—Celeste, my family, even her children when they eventually came to New York to visit—would joke about the reversal of names.

I remember the day I met her children, who had come for a holiday visit. Sitting in our living room on our elaborate crushed-velvet furniture, they appeared awkward. Yet they seemed to be filled with a sense of joy that I longed to touch. How exciting and special it was to have these people in the house. It was as if ambassadors had come from another land, yes, royalty! I was attracted to the rich, smooth darkness of their skin, and wondered how they perceived me and my dull white family. I also wondered whether they felt badly that their mother lived so far away from them, taking care of another woman's children.

I recall a song Celeste used to sing while she did the laundry, down in the basement:

> I'm sad to say, I'm on my way
> Won't be back for many a day
> My heart is down, my head is turning around
> I had to leave a little girl in Kingston town.

I would follow her around downstairs, helping with the laundry, singing along. I thought it strange that a girl should be singing about the sadness of leaving another girl. Now I can see that her sadness concerned her own children she had left behind. I too felt grief, though whether for her, for her children, or for myself who would also be abandoned—none of this was clear.

But grief there was when Celeste finally left. Actually, my parents fired her a couple of months after her children had come up north to live permanently with their grandmother in Queens, a few miles from our house. She had been pilfering groceries and liquor, bringing them to her family's apartment. Finally, after my mother had caught her "red handed," as she put it, bagging up steak, tuna, coffee, she was ordered to leave. There were some violent words between Celeste and my mother before Celeste ran down the basement steps to her room to pack. I followed her, saying, "I want you to know I don't care what's happened. I'm sorry you are leaving. I love you."

"I'm just glad to get out of this damned house!" she replied.

I was crushed—for although I had never felt real love from her, she had been the only person to attend to my needs. Maybe she never even liked me; perhaps it was impossible, given the circumstances and her alienation from her own children and culture. There was, however, an even deeper seed of bitterness between us, planted early on, a year after she had first come into my family.

It was 1956. I was in the tub for my nightly bath. I was never comfortable in the tub, having to view my own six year old body with its soft rolls of fat: stomach, belly, thighs. I liked to gaze into the water, astonished at the tiny bubbles that played upon the surface. Celeste washed my hair as I lay back with my head under the faucet, my hair hanging down toward the drain. She told me to sit up and washed my body with a soapy cloth: right arm, left arm, legs, back, front. Then she laughed, "Look at the water! Look at how dirty you are!" And yes, the surface of the water seemed to have a darkish film. When I responded, "Well, look at your skin! Look at how dark it is! I'm no dirtier than you are," she ran out of the room in a rage. There was an exchange between Celeste and my mother, until my mother stormed into the bathroom. While Celeste waited in the hallway, my mother slapped me over and over until my arms and face turned crimson. Later, my legs and back would turn black and blue.

That was 40 years ago. I don't often think of Celeste or the beating in the tub, but was forced to remember—and to begin to heal—yesterday. I had treated myself to one of the famous mineral baths in Saratoga Springs Park the evening prior to presenting a paper on Sylvia Plath and giving a poetry reading at the National Women's Studies Association Convention. At the Saratoga baths, the attendant assigned to me was a striking black woman. When she told me to remove my robe, when she took me by the hand to walk me naked over to the tub, I panicked. She gave me a questioning look, but continued, "You'll see a lot of dirt in the water. Don't worry, that's good dirt. The minerals pull it out of the body."

"That's good dirt?" I asked, wide-eyed and childlike, when she returned to take me out, wrapping me gently in moist, warm sheets.

"Yes," she smiled, "that's good dirt."

In a Time of Violence

Amityville, March 2, 2001

I am writing this under threat of a blizzard: already the snow is falling so profusely that I can't see the pond outside my door. Inside, I am warm enough, though wind gusts are beginning to cut through the fragile glass panes, chilling the room. Classes at the college are canceled, so I'll use this time and solitude to reflect on Eavan Boland, who will be coming to speak and read at the Sophia Center in April. The Sophia Center's mission is to foster dialogue about the sacred, the imagination, and culture. Two of Boland's books are on my coffee table: *Object Lessons*, a memoir, and *An Origin Like Water: Collected Poems 1967-1987*; I've been asked to write something for Sophia's newsletter, "Conversations."

Eavan Boland has also worked in solitude and in the cold, seeking to bring life and warmth out of the darkness, words out of flesh:

> No one's here,
> No one sees
> my hands
>
> fan and cup,
> my thumbs tinder.
> How it leaps
>
> from spark to blaze!
> I flush
> I darken.

What "leaps from spark to blaze" is the sacred imagination, rooted in the flesh, which enabled Boland to heal deep ruptures of spirit and body, woman and poet, humanist and scholar. And what appears as solitude is actually the self coming alive in conversation with the sacred, which often takes the form of a female spiritual presence who, as in "The Journey," leads her to an underworld of silenced women and children:

> I whispered, "let me
> let me at last be their witness," but she said,
> "What you have seen is beyond speech,
> beyond song, only not beyond love...

She is the "muse-mother," different from the presence she elsewhere calls the destructive "mimic muse" or "slut" who would have her recreate experience from a fabricated sexuality and unauthentic voice. Rather, the "muse-mother" is someone who "might teach me/a new language" until she can "speak at last/my mother tongue:"

> "...stand beside me as my own daughter
> I have brought you here so you will know forever
> the silences in which are our beginnings,
> in which we have an origin like water..."

※

In her memoir, *Object Lessons*, I read of her struggle to come to terms with a divided self: "woman" and "poet," what she calls "the stresses and fractures between a poet's life and a woman's." She describes her move from the city to the suburbs, a young married woman with children, trying to find language in the images, repetitions and rhythms of this altered and altering life: "the minute changes, the gradations of a hedge, the small growth of a small boy...a neighbor's dog would bark, then be silent. Maybe the daffodils which had been closed the week before would now be open."

Soon I find it difficult to stay connected to her words, for I am back with my own family, a young married woman and mother of an infant, having moved from New York to the suburbs of Long Island. The suburbs! Not a very "poetic place." Domesticity! Not, according to literary tradition, valuable as a subject of poetry. A woman? The object of a poem, but not, seriously, the subject.

It's not just the landscape that has changed. I am changing. My old attitudes, beliefs, the language I've learned so well. These tools no longer seem to connect me with myself and the world.

They are tearing me apart.

※

I pull myself out of memory and return to *Object Lessons*: Boland's absorption into the literary life of Ireland, her attempts to reconcile the personal and the political, her sense of isolation within a male literary tradition that had taught her so much. Too much? No, but perhaps had worked to silence her. "As the author of poems," she declares, "I was an equal partner in Irish poetry. As a woman—about to set out on the life which was the passive object of many of those poems—I had no voice. I had been silenced, ironically enough, by the very powers of language I aspired to and honored. By the elements of form I had worked hard to learn."

How to describe that love/hate relationship? Was the struggle to learn Latin—and all the male poets—a curse or a blessing when it came to using that beloved tool: *Language?* Or maybe it wasn't language and power that silenced women poets, but the "elements of form." Indeed, what are *the elements of form?*

Are these Eavan Boland's questions or my own? Suddenly, it doesn't matter. For I have brought my memories to her memories, and we're involved in an incredibly intimate, imaginative conversation. Which reminds me of the oral tradition—wherein the story and the story teller become part of the listener and the listener's story, passed down from generation to generation. It is this quality of the oral tradition embodied in a reconstructed feminist language that shapes Eavan Boland's poetry.

Her poem, "The Oral Tradition," replicates this process:

> I was standing there
> at the end of a reading
> or a workshop or whatever,
> watching people heading
> out into the weather...

She overhears the conversation of two other women who also remain in the room, lingering, talking. One of them is telling the story of her great grandmother, who had given birth in isolation:

> "she could feel it coming"—
> one of them was saying—
> "all the way there,
> across the fields at evening
> and no one there, God help her..."

Through the experience of listening, the speaker of the poem becomes part of the conversation, her listening itself creating a frame for the story. It allows her to enter the language, to become a part of it (as do I become a part of it, the reader of the poem, reading alone, in solitude, overhearing the speaker, who overhears the great granddaughter...).

While presumably, "only half-listening/staring at the night," soon "without warning/I was caught by it...the musical sub-text..."

> where she lay down
> in vetch and linen
> and lifted up her son

She calls this transformation through narrative "the oral song"

> avid as superstition
> layered like an amber in
> the wreck of language

Then, like Robert Frost, who had "promises to keep," the speaker declares that she "had distances ahead of me: iron miles/iron rails/repeating instances and reasons." Yet she stays connected to the conversation even while leaving, taking with her a sense of truth in new rhythms and images:

> the wheels
> singing innuendoes, hints,
> outlines underneath
> the surface, a sense
> suddenly of truth,
> its resonance.

This is the final (18th) stanza of the poem. The heart of the poem, however, is in its center, the ninth stanza, midway, that contains the "spark" of the sacred imagination:

> (Wood hissed and split
> in the open grate,
> broke apart in sparks,
> in a windfall of light
> in the room's darkness)

This is the only stanza of the 18 that is enclosed by parentheses, as if it is the core of a series of nesting eggs. It contains the central spark: the speaker of the poem, while listening to a conversation between two women (containing the story of one woman giving birth alone), is acutely aware of the fire and light.

She's "caught by it."

"It" could be the central core of a syntactically complex Latin construction.

"It" could also be Vesta's flame, the spark of the hearth, the "amber" in a "wreck of language."

"It" is the matrilineal connection passed from woman to woman within and despite a patriachal language.

And now it's as if I were sitting with her—and other women, perhaps—by a bright fire in a dark room on a cold winter night.

Rego Park, May, 1975

Things with Bob are getting worse. He's drinking a lot, harping on me constantly. He says that he considers me a part of himself; maybe that's why he treats me so badly—he's killing himself with all those drugs. But I'm starting to care about me, finding that the world is validating my intelligence and creativity, at least the academic world. And the feminist movement makes sense, the messages are getting through.

October 27, 1975

We're sitting at the small wooden table in the dining area of the apartment. I am looking through "Junction," reading the poems, including my own. Bob says, "it's our marriage or your career." His speech is slurred; he has taken a couple of tuinals.

"Then it's my career."

He leaves the apartment and doesn't return until about 3:00 in the morning, carried home by one of his drinking buddies, Danny. He has smashed a storefront window with his fist, says he pretended it was my head. The muscle of his right arm is hanging out, nearly severed; blood covers his shirt and pants. He is delirious. I try to stay the blood by putting the muscle back in his arm, tying it up with strips of shredded towels, while he eases the pain by pouring vodka on the gaping wound.

〰〰

4:00 AM. Danny and I convince Bob to go to the hospital. We get him into the car and drive a couple of miles down Queens Boulevard. At a light near the hospital, he jumps out, screaming that this is the hospital where his father died. This isn't true, but in his mind, the anguish must be so severe that he believes it. I follow him along the divider of Queens Boulevard as if I were tracking a wounded animal. When the police pull up, asking what is wrong, Bob freaks; as they approach him, he begins to kick and swing at them.

I watch as they push him against the car, pulling back his arms, the blood spilling on to the street. They handcuff him. Then they take him away.

≋

4:15 AM. I'm in a telephone booth on Queens Boulevard, waking up my father. "Bob's in trouble, he's been arrested."

My father takes care of it. He drives to the precinct and arranges to have Bob moved to a hospital, staying with him throughout the surgery. He will eventually get him off, telling the judge with unabashed humility that he is the defendant's father-in-law. My father will also put me on the witness stand to attest to Bob's good character. I will say that he's a loving husband.

October 28, 1975

I went to see Bob in the hospital this morning. He was out of surgery and awake. When I sat down on the chair by his bed, he looked at me with hatred in his eyes and said, "you did this to me."

Lindenhurst, New York, June 7, 1997

I went to see Bob in the intensive care unit this morning. He's still in critical condition, but at least they now know what it was: a heart attack. He is stable, eating, and in a few days they'll do a procedure to determine the extent of the damage. I'm feeling guilty. Yesterday he received the summons to appear in family court for a child support hearing. I have, all these years, constantly pushed for financial support for Karen; when he doesn't comply on his own, I take him to court.

When I left twelve years ago, I also left the house on the bay where we moved after Karen was born and where two years after that Tammy came into our lives. I met Tammy when she was 11. When her bike broke down outside my house, she asked to use the phone to call home. She stayed for a few hours playing with Karen, who was then two years old. Before she went home, we made a deal: she'd come over after school to occupy Karen while I got writing done. In exchange, I'd give her piano lessons.

After a couple of years, Tammy moved in with us and I began paying her, though it was impossible to measure an hourly pay. There were times she babysat, other times—especially during the crises that never seemed to end—she just stayed, keeping Karen occupied, out of harm's way. She became family to me, a daughter. I didn't push her to tell me what was going on with her own family, and her parents never came over or asked to meet me. Eventually she told me about the abuse, and by the time she was in high school, Tammy had taken her father to court and began receiving checks from him through the Department of Social Services.

It's been seven years since we left the house on the bay and moved to this house on the river; actually it's an estuary, but I like to call it a river. There's a small private beach at the end of the street that is deeded to the house where I sit for hours, thinking, reading, where I have been recovering pieces of myself.

Bob still lives in the house on the bay with his wife Marion. Why did he call me, and not his wife, when he woke up in the hospital after his heart attack?

I suppose I care about him, but I feel like his sister, that's all. I understand that he, like my mother, suffers from a disease, one that I didn't cause, can't control. When I got home today after seeing him in the intensive care unit, I went straight to my beach. The river was choppy, the sky spotted with dark clouds.

I'll get used to the house being empty. Soon Karen will be going away to college. Tammy was married and moved out a couple of years ago. I hope I can figure out how to buy this house, the landlord wants to sell.

Remembering Jane

Lindenhurst, 1984

I have been teaching—as adjunct, working on some poems and on the manuscript, *The Feminization of Form*. Last night I read an interesting essay, Rachel Blau DuPlessis' "The Critique of Consciousness and Myth in Levertov, Rich, and Rukeyser." These poets, she says, are responsible for the "invention of the re-evaluative quest myths...in which the act of critique guides the central acts of perception in the poems." Another way to describe this process is by speaking of archetypes and prototypes. She defines prototypes as "original, model forms on which to base the self and its action—forms open to transformation." An archetype, on the other hand, "is usually construed as an ideal form that establishes an unchanging pattern for all things of its kind."

Lindenhurst, 1992

Karen and I just got back from Mystic. We met my sister Denise and her kids Rebecca and Ben at a motel, spent the weekend eating, shopping, swimming. Saw a dolphin do tricks at the aquarium, though we in the audience were advised that these were not "tricks" but rather "behaviors."

In Mystic, I picked up the *New York Sunday Times* at a convenience store, which had updates on the abortion ruling. Roe v. Wade is being challenged, and we're waiting, like the rest of the country, for a decision from the Supreme Court. Over lunch, Denise and I started talking about Harvey, but the girls didn't want to hear about it. I'm terrified to think what could happen if abortion were no longer legal and safe. Karen is only 13, Rebecca 14; they take so much for granted.

≋

I finished the poem, "Abortion: 1962." I think it has helped me get some distance after carrying the images around with me all these years.

> A botched abortion and the whole world bleeds.
> Or so it seems to the doctor
> who didn't want to do it in the first place.

He had panicked when she died on the table.
So much blood he could not tell
the fetus from the woman.

So he kept on cutting, delivering
decisive strikes to the chest, finding
that the buzz saw carried from the shed worked best.

How hard was her skull.
How quickly did he gather, bag, and drag
the parts to the kitchen sink.

How does one stuff chunks of flesh
and length of bone down a long steel drain
where thin-edged blades

spinning like the law
that brought him to this madness
grind the matter down to soft pink pulp.

The earth, he prays, will heal this wound in silence.
He turns on the tap, washes the woman away.

♒︎

Writing comes out of our lives, our bodies, our accumulated experiences, which share associations and forms with archetypal experiences.

I could simply say that the woman in the poem was a victim of patriarchal power, of a culture that would not give her the right to choose; that denied her the power over her own body.

I could say that the images of her dismemberment and desecration are essentially a metaphor for the female principle that has been de-formed, denied, devalued and destroyed in women and men, and in myself.

And then I think of Susan Sontag's concept of illness as metaphor; and the reverse, metaphor as illness. Metaphoric thinking can itself become diseased. Keeps things stuck in comparison/contrast...cause/effect...polarity.

I must re-vise the metaphor: re-vise my thinking: loosen, undo, re-arrange.

♒︎

Her middle name was Jane, like mine. Part of my biography, mythology, my fate. Biography, not metaphor. Certain truths, realities, some imaginative fallacies. I must be careful not to lose my sense of humanity and my own self when I explore the deeper—also true—levels of meaning. I must remember to feel. And when I let myself feel, there is nothing but unending mourning, wrenching grief, incredible rage.

Barbara Jane was a human being, a young college student, who became pregnant. My mother says that Harvey swore he didn't initiate the abortion, that the parents gave her drugs to induce it, and Barbara was already hemorrhaging when she got to him. Harvey tried to save her.

Who knows what to believe. I've known other women who had abortions in the hands of Harvey, including my mother.

I do know that Barbara Jane's mother sat in the waiting room of Harvey's office while she died and was dismembered.

Skidmore College, Saratoga, June 1996

I am here at the National Women's Studies Conference in two roles. One, as an "academic" from Nassau Community College; I am to sit on a panel and read my paper on Sylvia Plath's "Three Women." I have a name tag that says, *Pat Falk, NCC*. I was also invited here as part of the Writers Series and will give a poetry reading Saturday night in the auditorium. The name tag for this role reads, *Pat Falk, Writers Series*. They have given me a room in a spacious condo where all the "writers" will be staying.

Laura Kaplan, who is also in the Writers Series, came in late last night. When she knocked on my door, asking me where the pillows are kept, we introduced ourselves. She wrote *The Story of Jane*, a book about the underground abortion network in Chicago in the 60's. We talked for hours, exchanging stories, and decided that tomorrow I will include the abortion poem in my half hour reading, followed by her reading from *Jane*.

Lindenhurst, July 25, 1996

Working on the poem, "On the Beach." Still having difficulty looking at the sky without seeing an airplane exploding. I heard about the crash of Flight 800 when I was up at Sid's in Amherst, the same day I read the new and old stories on Harvey. I'm having a tough time finishing the poem. Worked in the lines,

>Am I so much the child
>that I believe whatever blazes, dazzles
>is so utterly my own

that I deny my own perception,
lose the will to speak?

Writing as bearing witness, as speaking the truth, as bringing to form that which has been disintegrated. Writing as re-shaping, re-vising, re-forming.

The details themselves may not bring us to truth, but they make a configuration, a constellation. My own configuration: a cluster of associations that can put me in the roles of both victim and oppressor: ultimately, self-oppression.

An old image: Harvey, Barbara Jane, my mother, my father, myself, the scissors, the knife, the body parts, the garbage disposal, the newspaper clippings, doctors, my own disease, the battering, the cold distance.

As a woman-poet, com-posing, or putting together words, sounds, music, language, perceptions, I need to be able to imagine wholeness, to feel empowered, to live without threat. I need to reclaim my imagination, to find that voice that so clearly and with such authority said "I want to play the piano."

≈

Poetry—no matter how violent the content, no matter how terrifying or fragmented—because of its music, can integrate and heal; it can embody a vision of wholeness and peace. It is the cup: the bells, the dove, the heart.

≈

Re-arrange the paradigm. Change the rhythm. Take out one star, replace it with another. Shift. Draw a line that rises to another star: a line northeast along the paradigm; make a new design. Erase it, make another line, bring the curve down southwest; pull it up again, re-trace, re-shape. Let the third dimension take form: shade, color—red, blue, gold—texture. Open up the constellation. Let music in.

Jamaica Estates, July 11, 1971

Today I am to be married. Last night my bed broke, it just collapsed, crushing the boxes I've been keeping under the bed since my engagement party, boxes filled with household items, my books, things to take to the apartment.

I won't be taking the piano. It will stay here in my father's house. I have no room for a baby grand in the new apartment. Besides, I haven't played in years.

Rego Park, November, 1977

My Uncle Seymour called. He and my sister Adrienne are the executors of my father's estate. They have gone through his Will. My father specified three items, each one to be left to each daughter. Denise is to have the lace table cloth from Italy; Adrienne the antique desk; I am to have the piano. It's too big to fit in this one bedroom apartment, overcrowded with my books and Bob's plants. I guess I'll sell it, and use the money to buy a good typewriter, an IBM Selectric like the one I use at work. Maybe I can save up enough money from typing and editing to buy a piano. But now I need a typewriter to write my school papers.

Bayview Avenue, Lindenhurst, April, 1983

I will soon get the last settlement from my father's estate, something to the tune of $10,000. Bob says he is going to buy a boat. He's wanted one since we moved here on the bay. There is something else I want to do with the money: buy a piano. We're in a big house now, and it's time.

Bayview Avenue, Lindenhurst, August, 1986

I've counted eight boxes that I've filled with a few household items. I'm moving out, leaving Bob. There's not much I want to take. I'll be able to get this stuff over to my new place in my car. I'm moving only a mile away: I want Karen to be able to see her father whenever she wants, and I want to stay near the water. Tammy is going to her sister's.

Though I can manage most of my things on my own, I'll have to call professional movers to come for the piano. I haven't been playing much all these years, it just sat here, a reminder. But it's coming with me.

Park Avenue, Lindenhurst, December, 1987

Moving again. Must get out of this awful, cramped apartment. Found a house to rent on the water. Tammy's moving back in with Karen and me. There's lots of space, and a beach. The movers are charging extra for the piano. Who cares.

Riviera Parkway, Lindenhurst, June, 1994

Father's day, terribly hot, it reached 100 degrees. I went to my father's gravesite at Pinelawn this morning, then went home to cool down the house with air conditioners. Gary came at noon to take a picture for the book. He originally wanted to do it in his house, a studio shot, he said. No, I insisted that he come here and take the picture on my beach.

The title of my book is *In the Shape of a Woman*, from Rich's "Planetarium."

> I am an instrument in the shape
> of a woman trying to translate pulsations
> into images for the relief of the body
> and the reconstruction of the mind

I am at peace in this house by the river. It is here that I have returned to music. I have been playing for years now, mostly for myself, going back to old childhood pieces, learning some new ones. Karen and her friend Jessie used to dance and clap their hands while I played. Now Karen accompanies me with the violin.

When Gary got here, he asked me to play the piano. I was nervous, but I did. Then we went down to the beach and took the pictures for the book.

The Gilded Cage

> *Because women are outside the traditional canon, using formal*
> *devices is a way of taking a certain sort of linguistic power.*
> *For me, it's like entering the traditional "gilded" cage*
> *and inhabiting it instead of being locked up in it...I am taking*
> *that gilded cage and using it as a ribcage for my poems.*
> *I'm turning a trap into a place to breath from...in this way,*
> *formalism is feminism.*
>
> Molly Peacock

Lindenhurst, July 7, 1998

    The odor of insect spray lingers—a sweet, sickening smell. Gus, the landlord, sprayed it around the kitchen yesterday just before the soon-to-be owners and the engineer came over to inspect the house. I am not surprised that it sold so quickly. Anyone with an eye for beauty would fall in love with the view and the private beach at the end of the street; it's enough to make anyone overlook all the work that's needed.

    I have neither the money nor skill to take care of this house. Now, when I sit on the beach, grieving, I try to remember the many threats of living here, especially during the winter, during storms: the windows caving in from heavy winds, the oil burner shutting down, the frozen river breaking into monstrous chunks overflowing into the street.

    Does focusing on the negative help to let go of what you know you love? But if you look at the negative long enough, it becomes destructive. How much easier it is to destroy than to let go!

    I frequent the grounds of the new place in Amityville, laughing to myself that I have become a ghost that haunts a place before, not after, residing there. I walk along the grass by the lake, cross the bridge and watch the waterfall slide into the stream that meanders along the garden and under Merrick Road. The garden is filled with lilies and other flowers whose names I do not know but plan to learn. Sometimes I sit by the stream, imagining that my new neighbors can't see me, watching the leaves on the water carried by the current, the fish wiggle and dart.

    I am trying to learn to love the lake, which looks awfully shallow and murky. All sorts of growth dots the surface, odd looking plants poking out of the water, waving in the wind. Too much around the edges; unless it's cleared, the lake will turn to marsh. The water fowl include two adult and one baby swan, three ducks, four geese and a few goslings, one egret that

I watched circle round and round—and then take off—minutes before I drove to the attorney's office to sign the contract.

My unit is one of several small, charming attached townhouses. When I first looked at the place, I didn't like it. It seemed too small, and with the three vertically stacked floors it reminded me of a bird cage. The upstairs has two bedrooms; the ground floor a living room and kitchen; and the finished basement a study, laundry room, and storage. I feared I would feel trapped, that it would be impossible to orient myself to vertical space after the horizontal layout of the high ranch by the river: I would not be able to breath.

Still, it was the most space I could find on the water for what I could afford, and I eventually surrendered to the charm.

〜〜

I see a connection between the new house and my poetry. For the past few years, I've been working on what I call a "modified sestina": three stanzas of six lines, sometimes with a final stanza of three lines. Three stanzas: three floors: three basic segments of the human form (head, heart, pelvis). It feels as if I've been creating a structure and moving into it at the same time.

I'll have to learn to inhabit this house, my body, my language, without feeling trapped, without feeling caged. I need to feel *at home*.

〜〜

Buying this house is a political success for me. When I first tried to lease an apartment with Bob—the first place into which I moved after leaving my father's house—we were told we needed a co-signer. Bob and I were getting married, and when we applied to the rental management in Rego Park, they refused to consider my income because, they said, I was a woman. Furious, I had to ask my father to co-sign the lease. I recall them all (the managing agent, my father, Bob) chuckling at my frustration, my rage. Now I am negotiating on my own, buying a place with my money, based on my income, dealing with mortgage brokers, banks, lawyers, accountants.

〜〜

In this house I am also hoping to quit smoking. I need to learn to breath, and I will do so in my new bird-cage like house: by writing and by learning to sit quietly inside my own skin.

I must be able to live in layers of habitats: new habits, not addictions; *habere, to have; essere, to be*; to have—to birth—one's self while being one's self; to birth through ritual, habit, habitat, rhythm; a structure, a form in which/from which to breath.

City College, 1974

Adrienne Rich looked at me strangely today, after I sketched a pattern of triangles, what I called a "dialectical structure." She looked at me with that deeply questioning gaze she has, then asked me again what I planned to do after graduate school.

I felt like I held some kind of secret: a magic ball or cup or stone: something she saw in me, something I have hidden for a long time.

I still don't trust the cold abstractions, the symbolism, the hyper-intellectualism. Not because I'm afraid of my own power, but because it's so abstract that it threatens to take me out of my physical being. I think it's dangerous.

Okay, so I'm playing around with a dangerous theory. I drew for Adrienne a web-like connection of images that I have seen surface repeatedly in human consciousness: often connected, sometimes fragmented. The first, and most pervasive, is that of the hourglass—symbol of time, history, mortality, and the idealized form of a woman's body as perceived by the male erotic imagination.

In times of social and esthetic restriction, such as in the Victorian culture, the corset re-created the hourglass figure on a woman's body.

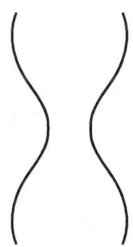

When men attempt to control or transcend time, mortality, the flesh—Woman—there tends to be a

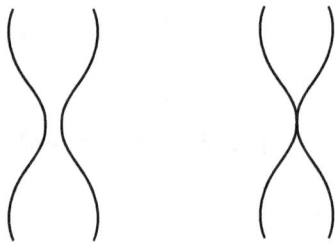

tightening at the center until the upper portion of the hourglass attenuates to a point merely touching the point of the lower portion of the hourglass. What remains are two triangles, one resting its tip upon the tip of the other. With sufficient force, the two sections become severed, fragmented, broken apart,

and they float out into space.

Embodied in this image and process is a triangular dialectic upon which is structured much Western thought. In Kabalic thought, and as Susan Friedman mentions in her book on H.D., *Psyche Reborn*, the triangle pointing downward is vaginal; the triangle pointing upward is phallic. The placement of these triangles—female on top of the male—presents a geometric statement about how the female can be perceived when in a position of power over the male; a response to this perceived power is penetration, rupture, and fragmentation at the center, which would otherwise open up and grow in a rounded, full, global image of pregnancy.

Sophia: where are you?

The other image I keep finding is simply the inverse of this: the diamond figure. Visually, it makes a statement: from unity, to duality, back to unity—a process M.H. Abrams describes in *Natural Supernaturalism* as a "fall from primal unity into self-division, self-contradiction, and self-conflict...the dynamic of [which]...is the tension toward closure of the divisions, contraries, or 'contradictions' themselves."

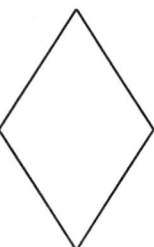

The image can be read horizontally or vertically. At its most tense and rigid, it embodies polarization (north, south, east and west). It is the symbol of perfection and like the diamond gemstone, is exceedingly valued. When softened, loosened, and relaxed, the sharp angles become arcs, turning into the infinite circle.

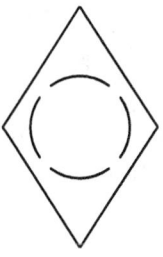

The arrangement of the triangles, as in the hourglass figure, is also hierarchical in nature. This time, it is the triangle pointing upward which rests upon the triangle pointing downward, or the male (phallic) over the female (vaginal). This figure can be read hierachically as the male over the female. It's much stronger, less vulnerable at the center to penetration and rupture than the figure of the hourglass.

After a while, it becomes difficult to separate and define these images and symbols, for indeed, they exist most often and most powerfully in human consciousness through interconnection. And, as is often the case, there are two significant ways these images have become connected: one in the form of the Mogen-David; the other in the form of dialectical networking.

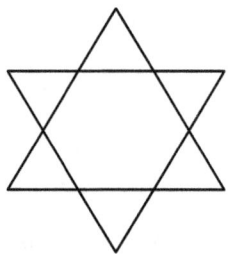

The Mogen-David is often regarded as androgynous:

Sophia: Where are you?

The triangle pointing up (male) and the triangle pointing down (female) co-exist in superimposition. Male and female connected this way seem to enjoy stasis, an equilibrium of sorts.

But as long as there are polarized associations—the attribution of *formative* agent with male, the quality of *passive matter* with female, this symbol deceptively implies unity, balance and harmony.

Lies.

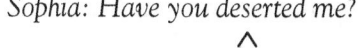

The other way that the hourglass and diamond—

Sophia: Have you deserted me?

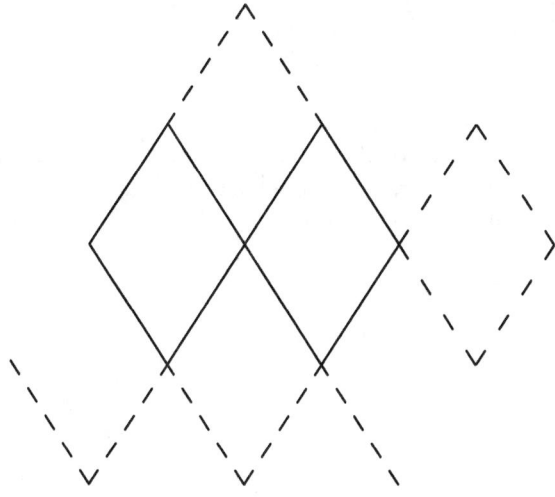

—have become connected is through the structure and process of *networking*: an addictive, space consuming web which is constructed and perpetuated through dialectical com-pulsion. Matter filling up space.

Compulsively. A material imperialism. Material-ism.

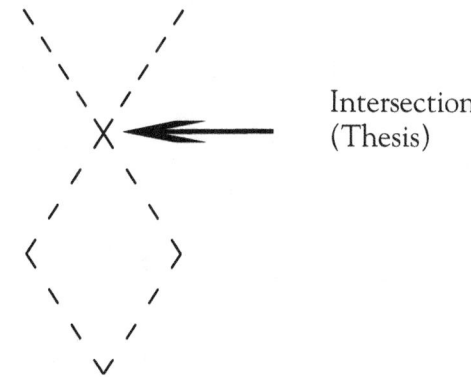

Intersection (Thesis)

The points of intersection are where thesis

Sophia knows nothing of this

and antithesis make a Hegelian synthesis, which becomes a new thesis from which springs its own antithesis, and so on. There is a rhythm to this process, difficult to intercept or break.

Feminist poets are interested in transforming this structure and process through changes in mythopoetic substrata: through myth, language, rhythm, image: by *transforming pulsations into images*. And it must be done through paradigmatic shifts.

≈

I drew the net-like, web-like structure for Adrienne. I said, "we have to live outside the structure, yet somehow work within it as well." I wasn't sure that I knew what I was talking about, but believed that somehow she did.

The Flow of Knowledge

> The flow of knowledge within the nervous system is not simple.
> *It does not travel back and forth so much as in a circle,
> simultaneously, mutually...This knowledge, interpreted by the
> central nervous system, and evaluated according to memory, old
> habits, present postures, attitudes, is transformed and sent back
> to the periphery as decision, commanding how the body will respond.*
> — Susan Griffin

June 18, 1997

Locate, find. Find in a particular place. The eye, open and closed; closing, opening. Behind the eye, a grey universe, planets, molecules; seeing outward, inward, no difference, resting and pulsing. Quiet of the morning: playing piano, writing. No longer wanting to write, just writing. Gone is the push, the will; still, there is discipline.

Looking over some essays, some to recast into the manuscript, I begin to feel that old fear that I can't combine the parts on women's poetry, teaching, my life. Must let it evolve. Fear too that time is limited. My sabbatical has officially ended, and I return to teaching in September.

I read over the essay on self-assessment and intimacy in the classroom that I had written for the active learning seminars. Then I wrote out by hand Lerner's definition of intimacy on a scrap of paper, taping it to the wall: "Why advocate intimacy in a writing classroom in the first place?" asks Joanne Campbell. "A crucial component of Lerner's definition of intimate relationships is the ability to stay emotionally connected to that other party who 'thinks, feels, and believes differently, without needing to change, convince, or fix the other.'"

Lindenhurst, 1981

Wisdom/Sophia is not intrinsically female. Sophia is a quality. As women have become devalued, so too has Sophia. As women are devalued, so too is wisdom.

To change the polarized structure and process, we must change attitudes and assumptions regarding gender; and to change attitudes and assumptions regarding gender, we must change the polarized structure and process.

It's that simple. And complex.

Prof. Stevens (I like him, I trust him) listened attentively to what I am doing, writing about. We met at his house in Brooklyn Heights to go over what I should study for the orals. Stevens is to be one of the examiners for my minor period in Medieval Literature, but he was interested in what my major work was on. We walked and leisurely talked along the promenade by the East River, the New York skyline looming on the other side. When I mentioned *the feminization of form*, and filled him in on my thinking and reading, he said that I've read enough—more than enough—but recommended one more essay: Eric Auerbach's "Figura."

Auerbach traces the first few recorded uses of the word *form (figure)*: "Originally *figura*, from the same stem as *fingere, figulus, fictor*, and *effigies*, meant 'plastic form'. Its earliest occurrence is in Terence who in *Eunuchus*...says that a young girl has a *nova figura oris* (unaccustomed form of face)... The following fragment of Pacuvius...probably dates from about the same period:

> *Barbaricam pestem subinis nostris optulit*
> *Nova figura factam...*
>
> (To our spears she presented an outlandish plague
> Fashioned in unaccustomed shape.)"

So from antiquity, *form*, as *figura*, was perceived, conceptualized and named in association with the feminine; it was further qualified as "unaccustomed," or strange; and because ambiguous, as a plague, a threat. Although Auerbach fails to notice the gender associations with *figura* in the first two uses of the term, he does raise an interesting point regarding the examples cited above: "Perhaps it is no more than an accident that in our two oldest examples, figura occurs in combination with nova; but even if accidental, it is significant, for the notion of the new manifestation, the changing aspect of the permanent, runs through the whole history of the word." Another traditional feminine quality embodied in the initial concept and word for form: changeable, mutable.

Unsteady perhaps? Necessary to control?

Auerbach follows the development of *figura* up through its radically different use in the Middle Ages. Prior to the Middle Ages, it was associated primarily with fiction, possibility and multiple dimensions: "dream image," "figment of fancy," "ghost," "atoms," or "bodies whose combination, motion, order, position...bring forth the things of the world."

According to Cicero, these "atoms" or "ghosts" are present both in the human body and the universe.

I'm imagining how it would feel, the atoms in my body connected to the atoms of the universe: constellation, interaction, easy peace.

※

Come the Middle Ages, *figura* became a mode of interpretation establishing a connection between two events or persons, the first of which signifies both itself and the second, while the second encompasses or fulfills the first.

This is known as *prefiguration*.

Sophia, or Wisdom, a female identified attribute of God, was eventually considered a prefiguration of the Old Testament's King David, who later was deemed a prefiguration of the New Testament's Christ.

Wisdom—clustered with other traditional "female" qualities such as intuition, the undefined and the mysterious—became culturally and historically supressed, replaced in importance by Logos, the traditionally male, logical, rational consciousness.

Polarization flung onto the continuum of time.

※

Has this temporal dualism in-formed humanity with massive addiction? If nothing is sufficient in itself, and must await fulfillment to be completed, what does it say about our ability to live fully in the present? To be satisfied with *what is*. Not to be or to have *more*?

And as this addiction moves farther away from Sophia toward Logos, where will it take us?

※

Suppose we were to shatter the structure, seeing it for the destructive, isolating misprison that it is: how to reconstruct the geometry? How to inhabit multidimensional space?

≈
≈

Suppose we were to simply *shift*, bit by bit, breaking out of the closed system of pre-figurative thinking while opening up space, gathering and re-forming constellations?

Heckscher Museum of Art, Huntington, New York, August, 2000

In a couple of minutes I'll have to get started: "Deeper Images and Rhythms," a writing workshop for artists and writers. Looking over the roster, I notice that all 12 participants are women. The table is set up in the center of the main gallery, surrounded by the work of Miriam Schapiro. After introductions and then some work on rhythm and images, I'll suggest that they write in response to the artwork. A plate on the wall describes one of Schapiro's collages: "*It's as if the secret geometry of the stars evolves into the origins of writing and thought.*"

Jamaica Estates, 1959

We have two canaries, both male and yellow, one with an orange blotch on its neck. Nobody gave them names. I wonder why only the male birds sing. They each live in separate cages in the living room, one on either side of the big window that overlooks the driveway. They sing while I play the piano.

Amityville, April 18, 2000

I pulled out an old Adrienne Rich book last night. It was 3:00 in the morning and I couldn't sleep. *A Wild Patience Has Taken Me This Far.* The poem "Integrity" has a passage that reached me in a way her poetry used to. Something about anger and tenderness existing not as polarities, but as two angels, or like the spider who knits and weaves in the same motion from one body. It's okay to be angry. It's okay to feel. And I won't smoke. It's 18 months since I've had a cigarette. The craving, withdrawal, it still feels like a "wild patience."

Rego Park, New York, 1976

I've been working on *The Feminization of Form*, examining poems of the great male poets. The sea imagery in Eliot's poem, "Marina" is lovely:

> This form, this face, this life
> Living to live in a world of time beyond me; let me
> Resign my life for this life, my speech for that unspoken,
> The awakened, lips parted, the hope, the new ships.
>
> What seas what shores what granite islands towards my timbers
> And woodthrush calling through the fog
> My daughter…

It's interesting that when Eliot refers to *form*, he associates it not only with the feminine, but with image, face, life, and the unspoken. Could Eliot have been perceiving that "unhatched egg," the silenced feminine principle, and re-forming that perception by "re-signing" the image?

And there's a bird, a "woodthrush calling through the fog."

Rego Park, July 28, 1979

I'm what's called "overdue" to give birth, according to doctors' calculations. I've been reading H.D.'s *Notes on Thought and Vision*, and am taken with her image of the jellyfish—an image of the emerging feminist sensibility, a globular form. I think we've since moved into the image of the starfish, its tentacles, like the petals of a flower, moving out in all directions.

Lindenhurst, 1994

I'm writing a review for *Women Artists News* on a book of poems, *Scaffolding,* by Jane Cooper who, at fifty years of age, speaks of "the poet with her torch of words in exile," "not at the source yet," but "finding her way home."

Scaffolding is divided into seven sections, six of which are selections of poetry—some published, some "reclaimed"—written from 1947 through 1983. The second section, a long, reflective essay, probes the political and esthetic context within which Jane Cooper struggled toward authenticity and integrity. When I first scanned the contents page, I wondered why the essay titled "Nothing Has Been Used in the Manufacture of This Poetry That Could Have Been Used in the Manufacture of Bread" (1974) was placed out of chronological sequence between the poems of Part 1 (1947-1951) and Part 3 (1954-1965). It became clear, after first reading the poetry, then returning to the prose of Part 2, that the essay literally replaces the years of silence and self-denial in this poet's writing life.

She struggled with that too familiar split identity, "woman" and "poet," seeking ways to transform experience. Her early studies in astronomy and physics inform her thinking in the early poems (1947-1951): a boy is born "head first, face down" into the violence of war and confining, patriarchal rationality of "Mercator's World," out of a "concrete womb with its round concrete walls." "Bitten by the tides of knowledge" the poet sees herself "imprisoned in the mirror," the "lady he wrote the sonnets to." While "Thinking of Kepler," who "gave himself over to his power" and "caged the sky," she raises the questions that will redirect her journey over the next 30 years:

> Where is the simple myth we used to have...
> That infinitesimal act, creation
> Which shocks two cells so that they melt and solve
> A riddle of light and all our darkness tears
> With meanings like struck water round a stone?
> Is it all gone? Are the meanings gone?

It became impossible to write between 1951 and 1954; the essay of Part 2 tells us why. It takes its title from a post war Paris department store window sign, "Nothing has Been Used in The Manufacture of This Furniture That Could Have Been Used in the Manufacture of Bread," substituting "poetry" for "furniture." This essay, generically compatible to Adrienne Rich's "When We Dead Awaken: Writing as Revision," Tillie Olson's *Silences,* and Virginia Woolf's *A Room of One's Own,* is a series of meditative explorations on why she wrote what she wrote when she wrote; why she did not; while unraveling often startling truths about the nature of a woman artist's life and work: her (non-participatory) role in World War II, believing that she was "writing a book of war poems from a civilian's, a woman's, point of view"; her sense of guilt, especially since she found the post-war "desolation...the bombed out landscape...virtually beautiful."

It would become important to understand this attraction even as she found herself "climbing the scaffolding of some new postwar housing because I was excited about architecture." The architecture of Self; of poetry; the furniture of sensibility would have to be rebuilt and replaced. What she had believed, for example, to be a woman's indirect treatment of war in her poems, she later understood as a metaphoric rendering of the condition of love, the "rapid wearing away of assumptions about what a love relationship should and can be between two people." The domestic realities of marriage and children may not, moreover, be the great inhibitor to our creativity; the tension may spring from an oscillating push-pull longing for/distrust of a patriarchally-determined sexuality and lifestyle and their interference in our work.

We also read of her study at Oxford and Princeton; the workshops with John Berryman and her bewilderment in "the company of poets," one of whom had told her that "to be a woman poet was 'a contradiction in terms'"; teaching at Sarah Lawrence; and finally, the New York City walk-up, "A Room of My Own, with Windows," in which she kept the journal that would give rise to a changed consciousness. The experiences and perceptions are rendered not as autobiography, but rather as threads of a tapestry which are pulled, tugged, examined, and re-stitched to form a prose piece that documents survival strategies of a women artist at mid-century. The journal "speaks of the necessity for changing myself, for finding a new style both of being and writing, to go with the changed realities I now perceived...it suggests that a new imagery must be found, less like a crustacean's shell. But to change one's images is like trying to revolutionize one's dreams. It can't be done overnight."

From the silence of those years emerged new imagery, rendered in looser forms, along with the central metaphor of "scaffolding," the place and method by which the woman poet can re-build imagination:

> All these dreams, this obsession with bare boards:
> scaffolding, with only a few objects
> in an ecstasy of space...How to begin?

While "toiling on houses," or new forms authentic to women poets, she must come to terms with isolation and old torn identities. She's "alone in a vast room/where a vain woman once slept...and still sleeps...trapped in my body," while "waiting...for some insight, some musical phrase."

By the final section of poems (1975-1983), she becomes "the poet with her torch of words in exile," "not at the source yet," but "finding her way home." By fifty years of age, she can praise her work: with both "earth" and "stone" she has "built a few unexpected bridges." The metaphor of scaffolding changes to "bridges," and finally to "threads," as if it is not the finished form that is critical, but the connections that continue to shape our identities and our lives.

In the closing poem, "Threads: Rosa Luxemburg from Prison" the poet speaks in the voice a woman who spent most of World War I as a political prisoner in German prisons. Based on Luxemburg's letters to her friend, Sophie Liebknecht, the poem exudes compassion, hope, and humanity by the juxtaposition of natural imagery against a tapestry of violence and isolation. Dualism is transformed to multiplicity issued from a central core, and the will to write prevails:

> Thus passing out of my cell in all directions
> are fine threads connecting me
> with thousands of birds and beasts
>   You too, Sonitchka, are one of this urgent
>   company
>   to which my whole self throbs, responsive
> Write soon.

My young student-poets at Nassau Community College readily acknowledge their sense of isolation in a violent world, yet the young women often insist they feel no "split" between "woman" and "poet." I say this may be the unconscious beast of denial; but if it is true, it is the result of poetic foremothers like Jane Cooper who have re-imagined a context within which women artists can create and connect from places of integrity and faith.

Inside, Looking

> *...don't look for me in a human shape.*
> *I am inside your looking. No room*
> *for form with love this strong.*
> *Rumi*

Jamaica Estates, September, 1966

The canary died. The last one; there it was on the floor of the cage. Must have been a draft. I used to have two birds, one by each window, on either side of my bed. Two males, singing away, just like the two canaries we used to keep in the living room. They'd sing when I played the piano. Only the males sing. I remember my mother telling me that. She was the one who bought the stupid birds in the first place.

When I stopped playing the piano, I lost track of the birds. They must have died. I don't remember how, when. Now these have died too. First the yellow one. A draft probably. And now the orange one, this one, lifeless on the floor of the cage. I kept the cage on the dining room table. Did I leave it dirty for too long? Did I forget to fill the plastic water container? Did I remember to scrape the greenish droppings off of the wooden bars?

I don't remember much, so much is fuzzy. Oh, their names were Peep and Cheep. Maybe the birds died only in a dream. Maybe I'll wake up and they'll be singing away. Maybe I never had birds. I'm fuzzy, but not in so much pain any more. Nice and numb. Nice and numb. Smoking kills the pain. Weird, though, it also helps me to feel. Hot sparks from long white sticks. Blue grey smoke. Little fire crackers.

I'll have to run outside the catering hall to sneak a cigarette during my sweet sixteen party, so my father won't see me. He beat me up for smoking a couple of weeks ago. Shit, my mother hit me all the time when I was little; now it's my father's turn. My mother couldn't deal with me as a child. My father can't deal with me as a woman. Too bad. I just bought a silvery metallic dress for the party. I also told Eric I want to have sex with him. He just tried a new drug, LSD. Maybe I'll try it too.

Amityville, January 13, 2001

Yesterday I drove with Karen along Ocean Parkway, our usual route, beginning with Robert Moses Causeway and over the bridge. How beautiful the bay looked, the waves frozen in motion, crystal, sparkling in the January sun. Then along the northern side of the parkway, traveling the bay, gawking at the trees bent and brittle, some naked and wiry, the evergreens full and full of color. Vanilla, deep blue, grey, ice-white. Finally up toward Jones Beach, along Wantagh Parkway and back home along Merrick Road. Karen remarked that she wished she had remembered to bring her camera.

"Maybe we'll go back tomorrow? Okay?"

So here we are again, this time traveling in a reverse path, first along the Wantagh Parkway, then leaving the car in the restaurant parking lot at Jones Beach. Karen didn't bring her coat, but she doesn't seem to care. Off she ran down the boardwalk and across the dunes to the edge of the ocean. It's freezing out there. I'm waiting in a small, glass enclosed restaurant, watching, amazed at her spirit, life, the glow in her when she holds that camera. I'm struggling to see her from this distance, fearing the waves will overreach her, take her out with them. Please, let her come back.

≈

She will come back: from the shore line, and again in a few months from school. Tomorrow she's driving back to Utica for the spring term. It's been a wonderful month with her home, despite some bickering and her remark that "we can't live together." Maybe we can't, or maybe we'll learn, or maybe she'll move, or I'll move, or... Of course she needs to do all the things young women are supposed to do. But what are those things? What is it that young women are supposed to do? What is it that she must do? What do I know?

≈

Only that I must let her go.

It feels like a tree is uprooting, its thick tentacles pulling up from the soil, out of my flesh, up and out of the earth.

Nassau Community College, Garden City, New York,
February 12, 2001

Read Mary Oliver's "Blackwater Woods" to my Modern Poetry students. Memorized one passage:

> To live in this world
> You must be able
> to do three things:

to love what's mortal;
to hold it

against your bones knowing
your own life depends on it;
and, when the time comes to let it go,
to let it go.

Jones Beach, January 13, 2001

Karen is crouched along the shore line. She looks like a shell, a mere crustacean.

Or a stone. Or a jellyfish. A brownish-grey smudge against a seascape.

Now I can't see her. But I believe that out there is my daughter, taking photos, alive, in touch, aware.

♒

She runs back up along the sand, across the boardwalk and in through the huge glass doors of the restaurant. She's flushed and out of breath, with dozens of shots in her digital camera. On the way to the car, she takes a photo of a gull on the edge of a roof. She asks my opinion, whether she should save it. In this crazy new camera, you see, you can delete or alter any image you don't like. Since she has only so much memory, she has to delete some—the ones she doesn't want—before she gets back to school.

I like the one with the bird, I say.

"But everyone takes pictures of birds." She is unsure, she doesn't know how talented she is. Or won't accept it.

"Yes, but look at the angle of the gull against the roof, the space between the bird's body and the wood, the color and lighting, it's a great shot."

We continue along Ocean Parkway, then I pull over to a shoulder and stop. Karen gets out and shoots a dune, then a perspective of the road. When she gets back in the car, we look through the images and keep some, delete others. The best is the one of the road, centered between bay and ocean, dunes and snow. It's full of contrasts—jagged frozen snow and smooth tarred asphalt, fuzzy dunes and clear sky, all zooming off and delineated in a rainbow-like geometry.

She tells me that she has words in her mind, the kind that I would put in a poem.

"What are they?"

"Snow-capped dunes."

"Nice. Maybe you can use them in your own poem."

We end up at Captree Boat Basin, where she takes a photo of the Fire Island Bridge, then has me pose against a sign that says *Had Enough?* We are laughing, and I'm remembering when I was eight years old, the times my mother had me pose for her practice shots when she was learning to be a photographer.

The world is swirling and nothing makes sense. My daughter is taking picture after picture, changing them in the camera. I tell her this is how you write poems. First rhythms, then images, and then you play with them, move the foreground, the background, clarify one thing, make another fuzzy. She looks at me as if she understands (accepts? honors?) the artistic bond we share.

Lindenhurst-Amityville, August 28, 1998

Moving day. How to leave the river?

The movers are taking out the furniture, piece by piece: couch, loveseat, tables, more boxes than I care to count. I sit on the beach, watching them load the truck. The objects are pebbles, the truck is a turtle, the sky a huge blue umbrella. I tell them that the first piece to go into the truck should be the piano. It has to be the last piece out of the truck and the last piece into the new place since it will stand on the wall just to the left of the front door.

Amityville, New York, July 29, 1998

Snuck into the Amityville town beach. You need a resident's pass to get in, and I'm not yet a resident. But the woman at the gate merely smiled, didn't check my ID.

Not many people here. Quiet. Small waves crawl up on land, then run back to the sea, leaving a dark wetness that feels like clay. The beach is not very big, a couple hundred feet, I would guess, the water protected by two long jetties that run out into the bay. A net connects the two jetties, keeping the swimming area free of fish and debris. There's a floating dock out in the deeper section with a three runged ladder bobbing in the bay.

I walk out into the shallow water: a few stray stones, not enough to hurt the bottom of my feet. Then soft sand, glorious water, light, waves, the sun beating down, the cry of the gulls. I swim out to the floating dock, climb the ladder and lay flat on my back with my face to the sun.

≈

I recall a dream I had, years ago when I was a student at City College. *I am having a tough time keeping afloat in the water, writing my honor's thesis on Adrienne Rich, working on Modern Literary Criticism with Sid, considering divorce, longing for family, for a daughter, for myself. Suddenly, there is Sid on a floating dock, a wooden life-raft of sorts, and I approach him while treading water. Can you help me? I don't need to speak this out loud. He hears. "Just keep swimming," he says. "Eventually you'll find your own life raft."*

Park Avenue, Lindenhurst, New York, 1986

My essay on Whitman came out in *The Mickle Street Review*. "Whitman's Mother Image: Feminist With Reservations." It was a revision of an old essay I had written at CUNY a few years ago for Angus Fletcher's seminar on 19th Century Poets: Swinburne, Whitman, Hopkins, Tennyson. In the Introduction, the editor referred to me as a *feminist*. I guess *feminist* is no longer a dirty word. I sent a copy to Sid. I've also sent a letter to Lillian Feder, I'm dropping out of the Ph.D. program.

A lovely poem, "My Father Saw Halley's Comet," appears on the page facing my essay. It's by William Stafford.

Bob called. He wants to see Karen. Karen and I are in a small one bedroom apartment, inland, where I've lined up all my bookcases in the center of the bedroom, nailing plywood to the back of each. In this way I've divided the room in two, half for me, half for Karen. But we can't stay here very long. I miss the water terribly. I circled an ad in the paper for a house for rent. It's on the water, a river.

Amityville Beach, New York, July 29, 1998

The sun's burning through the salt on my skin. How long have I been dozing, floating on this dock? My face to the sky, I imagine the stars up there, hidden behind the sun and blue sky. No, of course they are not *behind* the sky. It's a matter of faith. In the presence of light, I understand that darkness contains patterns. The universe is simply in place and moving. Light, position, perception.

Save yourself, others you cannot save. Adrienne Rich. As usual, her words rise to the surface. How they have sustained me.

And the words of others. And the passing of time. Looking up into the sky, imagining the hidden constellations, I recall a stanza from a William Stafford poem—was it the poem printed opposite my piece on Whitman? I remember reading it at a difficult time in my life.

> Time helps, the stars pulling apart
> their constellations and forming new
> meanings, the shapes of leaves imitating
> feathers at first, then paws, then wind prayers.

Notes

Prologue

the irony of many woman-made works... Donald Kuspit, "*Feminine Image*: The Representation of Woman In Modern and Postmodern Art," Catalogue to Exhibit, *Feminine Image*, Donald Kuspit Curator, Nassau County Museum of Art, Roslyn, New York, 1997, p. 40-43.

is there a connection between this state of mind... Adrienne Rich, "Notes Toward a Politics of Location," in Adrienne Rich, *Blood, Bread, and Poetry: Selected Prose 1979-1985* (New York: W.W. Norton & Co., 1986), p. 221.

negative capability... John Keats, letter to his brothers from Hampstead, December 21, 1817, Hampstead. Keats says that this is the quality that will "form a Man [sic] of Achievement, especially in Literature, and which Shakespeare possessed so enormously," in M.H. Abrams, ed., *The Norton Anthology of English Literature*, Seventh Edition, Vol. 2 (New York: W.W. Norton & Co., 2000), p. 889.

experimental...new kind of formal poetics... Annie Finch, "Introduction," *After New Formalism: Poets on Form, Narrative, and Tradition* (Brownsville, Ore.: Story Line Press, 1999) pp. xi-xii. and Annie Finch, *The Body of Poetry: Essays on Women, Form, and the Poetic Self* (Ann Arbor: The University of Michigan Press, 2005), p. vii.

living at the centre of every home... Jane Mills, *Womanwords: A Dictionary of Words About Women* (New York: The Free Press, 1989), p. 89. Mills quotes from Patricia Monaghan, *Women in Myth and Legend*, (London: Junction Books London, 1981).

According to this Necessity

nobody can counsel and help you... Rainer Maria Rilke, *Letters to a Young Poet*, H. Norton translation, 1934 (New York: W. W. Norton & Co., 1962), p. 12.

A Spy in the House of Ed

I begin thinking about... Susan Griffin, "The Way of All Ideology," Nanerl O. Keohane, Michelle Z. Rosaldo and Barbara C. Gelpi, eds. *Feminist Theory: A Critique of Ideology* (Brighton, GB: The Harvester Press Limited, 1982), p. 273.

female provides the matter...vital heat is included in semen... Aristotle, *Generation of Animals*, trans. A.L. Peck, p. 185 and MES [Medieval and Early Modern Science, by A.C. Crombie], p. 152, quoted in Susan Griffin, *Woman and Nature: The Roaring Inside Her* (New York: Harper & Row, 1978), p 8.

the brain is a great clot of genital fluid... Ezra Pound, "Introduction" to translation of *Remy de Gourmont's The Natural Philosophy of Love* (New York: Boni and Liveright, 1922), p. viii.

a masculine principle... George Dekker, *The Cantos of Ezra Pound: A Critical Study* (New York: Barnes & Noble, 1963), pp 42-43.

former image of matter... Carl G. Jung, "Approaching the Unconscious" *Man and His Symbols*, after his death by M.L. Franz (Garden City, New York: Dell, 1964), p. 95.

it is very difficult for a man... Herbert Read, *The Origins of Form in Art* (New York: Horizon Press, 1965), p. 133-137.

Eroticism is exciting... Shulamith Firestone, *The Dialectic of Sex: The Case for Feminist Revolution* (New York: Bantam, 1970), p.155.

our prevailing... Dorothy Dinnerstein, *The Mermaid and the Minatour: Sexual Arrangements and Human Malaise.* (New York: Harper & Row, 1976) p. 8-9.

as we explore the images... Susan Griffin, *Pornography and Silence: Culture's Revenge Against Nature* (New York: Harper & Row, 1981), p. 2.

we have to invent... Elizabeth Janeway, "Who is Sylvia? On the Loss of Sexual Paradigms," in Catharine R. Stimpson and Ethal Spector Person, *Women: Sex and Sexuality* (Chicago: University of Chicago Press, 1980), p. 19.

The Death of a Beautiful Woman

concerned with the feminist...in the past decade... Elaine Showalter, "Feminist Criticism in the Wilderness" Elaine Showalter, *The New Feminist Criticism: Essays on Women, Literature and Theory* (New York: Pantheon, 1985), p. 245-248.

shifting... I enjoyed a brief correspondence with Irena Klepfisz about the concept, the feminization of form, during which time she mentioned the importance of *shifting*. While I had already included the idea of shifting in the manuscript at that time, our conversations reinforced my thinking. I owe a great deal to Irena and her work.

the true feminist deals out of lesbian consciousness... Karla Hammond, "An Interview with Audre Lorde," in *American Poetry Review* March/April 1980, p. 20.

Anne Sexton's poems, "The Love Plant," "Words for Dr. Y," "The Twelve-Thousand Day Honeymoon," are from *The Complete Poems by Anne Sexton*. Copyright (c) 1981 by Linda G. Sexton. Reprinted by Permission of Houghton Mifflin Company. All rights reserved.

by the roots of my hair, Sylvia Plath, "The Hanging Man," *The Collected Poems*, ed Ted Hughes (New York: Harper & Row, 1981), p. 141

Sylvia Plath's "Three Women," was originally published in 1962, republished in *The Collected Poems*, ed Ted Hughes (New York: Harper & Row, 1981).

the death...of a beautiful woman... Edgar Allen Poe, "The Philosophy of Composition," in *The American Tradition in Literature*, Vol. 1, Bradley, Beatty and Long, eds. (New York: Grosset Dunlap, Inc., 1967), p. 892. Originally published *in Graham's Magazine*, April 1846.

The Madwoman in the Attic

women writers must kill the aesthetic ideal... Sandra M. Gilbert and Susan Gubar, *The Madwoman in the Attic: The Woman Writer and the Nineteenth-Century Literary Imagination* (New Haven: Yale University Press, 1979.), p. 17.

"Ay ma lad!"... D.H. Lawrence, *Lady Chatterley's Lover*, undated, third manuscript version, published in Florence in 1928 by Orioli (New York: Nelson Doubleday, Inc.), p. 215-216. See also D.H. Lawrence, *Lady Jane and Sir Thomas* (The Second Version of Lady Chatterley's Lover) (New York: The Viking Press, 1972).

Yeats, for example. . . Quotations from the "Crazy Jane" series are from the following poems, "Crazy Jane and the Bishop," "Crazy Jane on the day of Judgment," "Crazy Jane and Jack the Journeyman," and "Crazy Jane on God." M.L. Rosenthal, ed., *Selected Poems and Two Plays of William Butler Yeats* (Springfield, OH: Collier, 1966). On the naming of Jane: "Crazy Jane was modeled to some extent upon an old woman named Cracked Mary who lived near Lady Gregory. Yeats used her as a spokeswoman in a group of poems." Richard Ellman and Robert O'Clair, *The Norton Anthology of Modern Poetry*, Second Edition (New York: W.W. Norton & Company, 1988), p. 178. Jane Mills, in *Womanwords: A Dictionary of Words About Women* (New York: The Free Press, 1989) also refers to Jane as "every-woman," a generic form. The importation of the Celtic associations is significant, accounting for much of Jane's political and feminist orientation.

used to live in Gort... Monaghan, Patricia. email correspondence to Pat Falk, October 31, 2003.

Aha, TAM LIN!... Patricia Monaghan, email correspondence to Pat Falk, November 2, 2003. See also Patricia Monaghan, *The Redheaded Girl from the Bog: The Landscape of Celtic Myth and Spirit* (Novaco, Ca.: The *New World Library*, 2003) as well as R.J. Stewardt's website reference 19; http://tam-lin.org/version/steward.html

late in the spring, they picked a name... Laura Kaplan, *The Story of Jane: The Legendary Underground Feminist Abortion Service* (New York: Pantheon, 1995), p. 27.

Jane is Everywoman... Kathleen Spivack, *The Jane Poems* (New York: Doubleday & Company, 1974), introductory page (unnumbered).

Jane Marcus, "Storming the Toolshed" in N.O. Keohane, M.Z. Rosaldo, B.C.Gelpi, *Feminist Theory: A Critique of Ideology* (Chicago: University of Chicago Press, 1981), p. 217-135.

Alicia Ostriker, *Stealing the Language: The Emergence of Women's Poetry in America*. (Boston: Beacon Press, 1986). Ostriker's work and this book in particular have been of tremendous value as I struggled with my own polarized sensibility. It was not until I had the opportunity to personally speak with her, however, that I understood the importance of accepting my biological connection to my mother. She said that to come into our own as women poets, it is essential to accept the connection to our mothers, no matter how difficult. This was in 2001, in Huntington, New York. A few months later, I heard her repeat that message in a talk at Poets House in New York.

Today Life Opened Inside Me

"Anne Sexton was a poet and a suicide." Adrienne Rich, Memorial talk for Anne Sexton, City College, New York, October 5, 1974; later published as "Anne Sexton: 1928-1974," in Adrienne Rich, *On Lies, Secrets and Silence: Selected Prose 1966-1978* (New York: W. W. Norton & Company, 1979).

the annunciation that founded Greece... William Butler Yeats, *A Vision* (New York: The Macmillan Company, 1956), p. 268.

Unfolded out of the strong and arrogant woman... Walt Whitman, "Unfolded Out of the Folds," in *Leaves of Grass*, first published in 1856, under title of "Poem of Women," in 1860 as No 14, in *Leaves of Grass*. The edition from which this passage is taken is Emory Holloway, ed. *Leaves of Grass* (New York: Doubleday & Co., Inc., 1926), p. 326.

It is I, you women, I make my way... Walt Whitman, "A Woman Waits for Me," in Emory Holloway, Ed., *Leaves of Grass*, (New York: Doubleday & Company, Inc., 1926), p. 87.

form beyond forms... Denise Levertov, "Some Notes on Organic Form" in *The Poet in the World* (New York: New Directions, 1960), p. 7. See also "A Further Definition" and "Work and Inspiration: Inviting the Muse," also in *The Poet in the World*.

Passages from Denise Levertov's poems are in the following collections: "Growth of a Poet" and "Song for Ishtar," in *O Taste and See*, New Directions Publishing Corporation, New York. p. 3. "Cancion" in Denise Levertov, *The Freeing of the Dust*, New York: New Directions, 1978, p. 49. For permission credits see acknowledgements page; permission provided by New Directions Publishing Company.

Passages from Anne Sexton's poems, "Somewhere in Africa," "The Horoscope Poems," and "The Fierceness of Female," "Live," from *The Complete Poems by Anne Sexton*. Copyright (c) 1981 by Linda G. Sexton. Reprinted by Permission of Houghton Mifflin Company. All rights reserved.

the sun, a traditionally masculine source of power... I am using the word "traditionally" to suggest only that it has been an association internalized by our culture and literature, though as Patricia Monaghan points out in her book, *O Mother Sun!* (Crossing Press, 1994), the sun has in other times and cultures been perceived as female.

A Life I Didn't Choose

a life I didn't choose... Adrienne Rich, "The Roofwalker" in *Snapshots of a Daughter-in-Law: Poems 1954-1962* (New York: W.W. Norton & Co., 1967), p. 63.

what the cluster of scholars... Janet Emig, "The Tacit Tradition: The Inevitability of a Multidisciplinary Approach to Writing Research," in Janet Emig, *The Web of Meaning: Essays on Writing, Teaching, Learning, and Thinking*, ed. Dixie Goswami and Maureen Butler (Upper Montclair, N.J.: Boynton/Cook, 1983), p. 147-148.

when a theory is transformed... Susan Griffin, "The Way of All Ideology," in Nanerl O. Keohane, Michelle Z. Rosaldo and Barbara C. Gelpi, eds. *Feminist Theory: A Critique of Ideology* (Brighton, GB: The Harvester Press Limited, 1982), p. 280.

when people of a group share an oppression... Claudia Tate interview, "Audre Lorde," in Claudia Tate, ed., *Black Women Writers at Work*, (New York: Continuum, 1983) p. 101-102.

I thought about Celeste yesterday... Section on Celeste, the NWSA, and the mineral baths was originally published as the memoir, "*I Had to Leave a Little Girl*," in Barbara Blouin, editor, *Like a Second Mother: Nannies and Housekeepers in the Lives of Wealthy Children* (Halifax, Canada: Trio Press, 1999).

In a Time of Violence

Eavan Boland, *Object Lessons: The Life of the Woman and The Poet in Our Time*, (New York: W.W. Norton & Co., 1995). p. 113, 173, 114,

Eavan Boland, *An Origin Like Water: Collected Poems 1967-1987* (New York: W.W. Norton, 1996). Poems quoted: "Solitary;" (p.100); "The Journey" (p. 184); "The Oral Tradition," p. 160-162.

Remembering Jane

invention of the re-evaluative quest myths... Rachel Blau DuPlessis, "The Critique of Consciousness and Myth in Levertov, Rich, and Rukeyser," in Sandra M. Gilbert and Susan Gubar, ed., *Shakespeare's Sisters: Feminist Essays on Women Poets*, ed. (Bloomington: Indiana University Press, 1979) p. 280-281, 299 (the later quote is DuPlessis' of *The American Heritage Dictionary* at the word "ideal").

am I so much the child... from Pat Falk, "On the Beach," in Robert McGovern and Stephen Haven, *And What Rough Beast: Poems at the End of the Century* (Ashland, Ohio: The Ashland Poetry Press, 1999), p. 54.

Adrienne Rich, "Planetarium," in *The Will to Change: Poems 1968-1970* (New York: W.W. Norton & Co., Inc., 1971).

The Gilded Cage

because women are outside the traditional canon... Molly Peacock, interview by Kevin Walzer, *AWP chronicle*, Oct/Nov. 1996, p.3. See also Peacock's essay, "From Gilded Cage to Rib Cage," in Annie Finch, ed. *After New Formalism: Poets on Form, Narrative, and Tradition* (Ashland, OR: Story Line Press 1999), p. 70-78.

Susan Friedman, *Psyche Reborn: The Emergence of H.D.* (Bloomington: Indiana University Press, 1981), p. 276. For other renditions of this triangular process, see Yeats, *A Vision, op cit*; any of the available diagrams of the Kabala's Tree of Life; and Picasso's *Standing Nude with Clasped Hands (Proportion Study)*. Paris, April-May 1907. Pencil and black ink on page from Daumier exhibition catalogue, Seckel, carnet 5, p. iv. Private collection. Reprinted in Pepe Karmel, *Picasso and the Invention of Cubism* (New Haven: Yale University Press, 2003), p. 57. See also Susan Griffin's discussion of these symbols and the appropriation of the Mogen-David by Hitler in *Pornography and Silence: Culture's Revenge Against Nature* (New York: Harper & Row, 1981).

M. H. Abrams, *Natural Supernaturalism: Tradition and Revolution in Romantic Literature* (New York: W.W. Norton & Co., 1973), p. 255. Abrams continues that the "beginning and end of the journey is man's ancestral home, which is often linked with a female contrary from whom he has, upon setting out, been disparted. The goal is...often signalized by a loving union with the feminine other, upon which man finds himself thoroughly at home with himself, his milieu, and his family of fellow men." p. 255. This perspective both alienates and objectifies the female principle, assuming that she passively waits for union with the questing male.

The Flow of Knowledge

the flow of knowledge, Susan Griffin, *A Chorus of Stones: The Private Life of War* (Woodston, UK: Anchor Books, 1992), p 269.

why advocate intimacy in a writing classroom... JoAnn Campbell, "Controlling Voices: The Legacy of English A at Radcliffe College 1881-1917," *College Composition and Communication* Dec. 1992. Vol. 43 #4; 472-485; quotation p. 480-481.

Originally figura, *from the same stem...* Eric Auerbach, "Figura" in *Scenes From the Drama of European Literature: Theory and History of Literature 9*, tr. Manheim (Manchester: Manchester University Press, 1984), p. 11-12, 13-76.

Miriam Schapiro Exhibit, Heckscher Museum of Art, Huntington, New York, Summer 2000. Wall text for *Orion #2*, (1984) acrylic, Courtesy of Bernice Steinbaum Gallery, Miami, Florida: "The title...suggests a constellation. Against a symmetrical stage backdrop (here empty of dancers), Schapiro distributes patterns of dots. While sharply focused against the other arcs, they gradually blur and become more random in pattern as they enter the empty stage. It's as if the secret geometry of the stars evolves into the origins of writing and thought."

Rich, Adrienne. "Integrity." *A Wild Patience Has Taken Me This Far: Poems 1978-1981* (New York: W.W. Norton & Co., Inc. 1981).

T.S. Eliot, "Marina," in T.S. Eliot, *Collected Poems 1901-1935* (New York: Harcourt, Brace and Company, 1936), p. 131-132.

H.D. *Notes on Thought and Vision* (San Francisco: City Lights Books, 1982).

Jane Cooper, *Scaffolding: Selected Poems* (Gardiner, Me.: Tilbury House, 1993). Section on Cooper originally published as review, Pat Falk, "Review of Jane Cooper's Scaffolding," *Women Artists News*, Midmarch Arts Press New York, New York 1994. Poems quoted: "All These Dreams," "March," "Threads: Rosa Luxemburg From Prison," "After the Bomb Texts," "Praise," "For a Boy Born in Wartime," "Long View From the Suburbs."

Inside Looking

don't look for me… Mowlana Jalaluddin Rumi, *The Essential Rumi*. Coleman Barks with John Moyne trans. (San Francisco: Harper Collins, 1995), p. 139.

Mary Oliver, "Blackwater Woods" in *New and Selected Poems*, (Boston: Beacon Press, 1991), p 178.

"Save yourself; others you cannot save…" Adrienne Rich, "Snapshots of a Daughter-in-Law," in *Snapshots of a Daughter-in-Law, Poems 1954-1962* (New York: W.W. Norton & Co., Inc., 1967), p. 21.

William Stafford, "My Father Saw Haley's Comet," *The Mickle Street Review*, Number Eight: The Proof of a Poet, The Walt Whitman Association, Geoffrey M. Sill, ed., 1986, p. 46.

About the Author

Born in 1950, Pat Falk grew up in New York City, eventually moving to the south shore of Long Island. She was educated at the City University of New York and is currently a professor of English at Nassau Community College in Garden City, New York where she teaches writing, literature and women's studies. She has received awards for both her poetry and scholarship: from the National League of American Pen Women, The Unterberg Poetry Center, the Writer's Voice, and *Black Bear Review;* she has also received an Edward C. Mack Memorial Fellowship and a Faculty Distinguished Achievement Award. Her other books include the poetry collections, *In the Shape of a Woman* and *Sightings: Poems on Discovery*. She maintains a website www.patfalk.net.

From Reviews

It Happens As We Speak: A Feminist Poetics

"Fascinating, quest-like, moving around in an unknown landscape."
—Patricia Monaghan, author of *Red-Haired Girl From the Bog*

"I read the book in one sitting, I was so moved by it. Most important, it's about the process of discovery. It's about questioning and working toward change. Her personal transformations become her best teacher about poetry, especially showing what it means to write as a woman."
— Pramila Venkateswaran, author of *Thirtha*

"Tumbling from Adrienne Rich to Charlotte Bronte and back again, Falk explores the inner workings of why a scholar makes her choices and how a poet can feel that her life is both endangered and rescued by the art she practices."
—Molly Peacock, author of *Cornucopia*

"A mixture of nonlinear biography, poetry, literary criticism and symbiotics. Falk uses a mixture of previously separated writing forms to cross what she sees as an arbitrary line between the personal and the professional in writing. Each category informs the other in a way that carries forward the thoughts of the writer."
—Ian Wilder, *Long Island Pulse*

"A prototypical vehicle for travel through interior space."
—Daniela Gioseffi, author of *Women On War: International Writings* from the Feminist Press.

In the Shape of a Woman

"Written with a quiet fortitude...a graceful testament to the pleasure, pain, and endurance of a contemporary woman. Falk brings us into her world with raw, gutsy detail and without apology."
—*Book/Mark*

"Falk elevates the concept of feminism to one of humanism...[her] work speaks to the heart of anyone who views their life as a continuing process

of conscious refinement."
—*Long Island Update*

"What the attentive reader feels is an ethereal sense of intimacy—an almost ineffable identification with the persona's humanity...the writer artfully commands our unreserved confidence."
— *New York Beacon*

"Truly breathtaking and erotic and real."
—Regie Cabico

www.ingramcontent.com/pod-product-compliance
Lightning Source LLC
Chambersburg PA
CBHW071004080526
44587CB00015B/2339